Praise for *Designing Courses and Teaching on the Web*

"As an online instructor I am calmer and increasingly confident knowing I have this text to guide and mentor me through the designing and implementation of my online learning curriculum." —**Billie Jempty**, account executive, Apple Learning Interchange

"Drawn largely from the successful and effective Pepperdine OMAET program, Fisher provides real world case studies and scenarios to help illustrate the models and theories presented. [The book] includes tools for course interaction and engagement; recommendations for web page design, accessibility and usability, communication, and facilitation techniques; a best practices checklist, and constructivist theory." —**Sarah Bordac**, project manager, Center for Media Literacy

"A major challenge for Web-based learning designers today is to find new and out of the ordinary ways to take curriculum that has been taught in the classroom and transform it into engaging and effective online courses. Professor Fisher has drawn from her vast wealth of knowledge and experience along with the latest research and shares with her readers 'how to' successfully maximize technology's tools to allow the learner to be actively involved in the learning process while constructing their own understanding to produce the highest level of learning possible." —**Mary Anne Campo**, coordinator, staff technology development, District 81-Spokane, Washington Public Schools

"The challenge of continued professional development for teachers and corporate trainers today lies not only in finding fresh ideas, but the time to examine and prove them out with others facing similar challenges. Dr. Fisher walks us through the art and science of creating an environment where learning is facilitated online by bringing professionals from around the world together in collaboration. She takes the trendiness out of online learning and replaces it with grounding in solid constructivist theory." —**Kathy Milhauser**, Nike Training Manager

"Mercedes Fisher will make you stop and think about possibilities—guidance, intuitiveness, understanding and trust in the process. I recommend this book and hope that it will inspire you and others to make a difference." —**Ana Guenthner**, education department, California State University

"While most books on this topic offer little more than advice on creative ways to post existing course content to the Web or a learning management system and then slap on an assessable online discussion, Fisher introduces you to an entirely new course model for online education, one that has been field-tested and proven overwhelmingly effective. This book is a must-read for anyone serious about creating positive learning outcomes online." —**Patrick Douglas Crispen**, academic technology consultant, CSUF Faculty Development Center

"A clear vision and blueprint for designing rewarding Web-based learning experiences. Dr. Fisher provides an invaluable trove of resources for the online instructor, covering everything from design, content, and pedagogy, to the all-important development of community and effective use of synchronous learning tools. . . . Moreover, the author explains how to design a virtual learning environment where the quality of social relationships formed can exceed those created in the traditional classroom experience. . . . Teachers and trainers alike will benefit from Dr. Fisher's expertise in Web-based course development and recognize why she is rapidly becoming an internationally sought out and renowned expert in Web-based learning design and delivery." —**Derek E. Baird**, director of education and training, People Staffing Services

"[Fisher] wonderfully illustrates the reasons why this model and others like it are so successful. Through a comprehensive blueprint, she takes the reader through all phases of creating a rich online learning environment. The model has benefited the school district I work at in countless ways. For anyone who has ever been curious about learning online, I highly recommend this book." —**Randy Hollenkamp**, technology resource teacher, Evergreen Elementary School District

Designing Courses and Teaching on the Web

A "How To" Guide to Proven, Innovative Strategies

Mercedes Fisher

ScarecrowEducation
Lanham, Maryland • Toronto • Oxford
2003

Published in the United States of America
by ScarecrowEducation
A wholly owned subsidary of the Rowman & Littlefield Publishing Group, Inc.
4501 Forbes Boulevard, Suite 200, Lanham, Maryland 20706
www.scarecrowpress.com

PO Box 317
Oxford
OX2 9RU, UK

British Library Cataloguing in Publication Information Available

Library of Congress Cataloging-in-Publication Data

Fisher, Mercedes M.
   Designing courses and teaching on the Web : a "how to" guide to
proven, innovative strategies / Mercedes Fisher.
      p. cm.
   "A ScarecrowEducation book."
   Includes bibliographical references and index.
   ISBN 1-57886-052-0 (pbk. : alk. paper)
   1. Teaching—Computer network resources. 2. World Wide Web.
3. Computer-assisted intruction—Design. I. Title.
LB1044.87.F57 2003
371.33'44678—dc21   2003007582

Contents

Preface

Dear Prospective Course Designer and Instructor:

Interactive learning, online collaboration, knowledge sharing, project-based learning, future-thinking faculty, technology supported curriculum, and program innovation—these need to be terms associated with our courses for the year 2004 and beyond. As a teacher, I realize there should be a better way of training instructors and course developers. I spent years researching learning theory, technology, and social communities and as a result, I came to believe it was time I started studying how students learn more efficiently in web-based environments. This started me on my journey of how people learn in online settings.

Most research and articles on distance or online education are unclear or nowhere is there anything noted about the teaching methodology used in the online environment. I was troubled by this and began to look at things such as, what do "good" instructors do and what are some interesting classroom practices that can and should be happening in an online environment. In the Pepperdine Online Masters of Education Technology, we explored exactly these types of issues, as we were willing to put ourselves under the microscope. Familiarity with the community is an important dimension of any kind of membership in a community of practice. The researcher's continuous participation within the environment allows her to observe how the participants apply meaning and are motivated within the online environment. Findings, conclusions, and recommendations from this study make it possible for educators to develop strategies as they implement online collaboration. We continue this discussion and share instructional strategies and our experiences with pedagogy in an online environment in this book.

The framework presented in the following chapters, provides an excellent scaffold for instructors to base their web-based instruction on. We particularly focused on pedagogical strategies. The information presented in the illustrations and examples are invaluable tools to assist a developer or teacher. We have tested and revised the suggestions for instructional strategies, guidelines, rubrics, and plans for implementation. Using these ideas, you won't need to brainstorm so much in future course development projects.

The question is when will teachers and course designers have time to master these strategies? We believe that the time is now! We support the thinking that successful online courses must become systematic, even organic. Soon, education will no longer be defined by static guidelines but rather by growing, changing, and evolving sets of opportunities, technologies, projects, and people. What we know, are willing to try, and have access to, will determine our ability to prioritize, focus, and teach students in the future. The use of technological tools in education will be the soul of the new information society in the digital age. The future is here and we encourage you to embrace it.

Illustrations

Tables

Acknowledgments

Once again there are many people who ought to be thanked profusely for helping this book become a reality, only a handful of whom can be mentioned here.

Many thanks to my hundreds of students for teaching me how to effectively teach people online through vital feedback and guidance. Thanks to the entire team at the Graduate School of Education at Pepperdine University, especially Linda Polin, Gary Stager, and Cara Garcia for their many valued forms of support over the years. Their commitment to education and belief in learning communities has made this book possible. Thanks to Greg Thompson, Dave Tucker, Nancy Smith, Bonita Coleman, and Kyle Ekberg for sharing their expertise and experience about online teaching and learning, as well as reviewing portions of the book for content and usability. You all truly deserve the title "critical friends."

Special recognition goes to Peita Ramos and Kathy Cronin for their substantial organizational support and collaboration.

Thanks to Adam Spelbring for the cover photo. And thanks to my sons, Jake and Austin, for your patience and inspiration while I worked on this project. You are wonderful, invaluable, and dear. Thank you.

Introduction

> I entered the classroom with the conviction that it was crucial for
> me and every other student to be an active participant, not a pas-
> sive consumer . . . [a conception of] education as the practice of
> freedom. . . education that connects the will to know with the will
> to become. Learning is a place where paradise can be created.
>
> —bell hooks, Women's Voices: Quotations by Women

Educational institutions have rushed to provide online courses; however, too often schools have discovered the difficulty in transferring
effective teaching strategies from the classroom to an online environment. There is no doubt that the educational use of online technologies
will grow. The challenge for instructors and institutions is how to create educational experiences for students that enhance learning and take
advantage of the inherent capacity of the World Wide Web.

A unique aspect of quality online courses is how they rely heavily on
effective collaboration to create a meaningful learning environment.
Learning online can be optimized when it happens with others. Unfortu-
nately, online collaborative instruction is not as simple as replicating the
community atmosphere that is found in the traditional brick-and-mortar
classroom. Recently, however, there has been a swell in research about
the web and how people learn. If technology has the potential to transform learning experiences, how do online learning environments need to
differ from more traditional approaches in order to be successful?

Educators are likely to be successful if they take advantage of the
opportunities afforded us by new technologies. Easy-to-use tools and

interface enhancements already exist alone or as parts of courseware platforms. These offer new extended educational opportunities for instructors to explore, build, and teach their courses with richer content and within a "more realistic" context.

Some examples of these new capabilities include:

- real-time chat tools
- visually integrated notes and advanced hyperlinking
- simplified template development and integration
- electronic library resources
- private rooms for synchronous and/or asynchronous group work
- knowledge-building tools like interactive digital whiteboards
- three-dimensional concept visualization tools for modeling and navigation
- streaming video/audio and slide show with audio capabilities
- animations or other forms of multimedia
- tools for providing feedback and tracking performance
- more powerful search engines

Teaching faculty and students basic computer skills is not enough to bring about the pedagogical change needed to take advantage of web-based opportunities. Faculty and students need to learn about collaborative strategies and uses of technology so they have the knowledge and skill to integrate these strategies into course-based experiences.

Students are increasingly Internet savvy and application enabled. Because of this they become bored quickly with "page turning" assignments that mimic typical print work. The challenge for teachers is to use the technology in new and unique ways instead of just trying to recreate traditional lessons. "Shovelware" is widespread in today's online courses. Instead of making a pedagogical change in delivery, a teacher simply "shovels" current content into a new container (A. B. Fraser, 1999, b8). Like, Arthur C. Clarke, we agree that information is not knowledge, knowledge is not wisdom, and wisdom is not foresight. Each grows out of the other and people need them all.

Educational psychologist William Glasser's research on learning modes demonstrated that people typically retain 80 percent of what they learn when experiencing the content. When we design and deliver learning experiences that actively involve students in the creation of their own knowledge, learning will be enhanced. This will allow faculty and students to experience innovative technology–supportive learning environments.

This user-friendly guide will reveal important information and insight to assist faculty in designing, creating, adapting, and integrating good teaching and successful learning with effective use of new online tools at any developmental level, in any context. We will explore and examine new ways to give information to students, teaching ways that will work easily, quickly, and with better long-term results. We will share our best strategies for delivering meaningful courses and avoiding common barriers. This detailed resource book provides a mix of professional expertise and real-life experience to enable the successful integration of hands-on technology and practical guidance on Web-based strategies for learning. To create a better user's experience, instructors must help students understand that their program uses the tools that are available to create both a social and technical infrastructure for learning. They should be aware that to do this, the faculty has to look at different systems, talk about them, experiment with evolving systems, and accept a different conceptual view of learning.

We will share the efficacy of our current model. To make our book user friendly we have included examples, guides, and easy-to-follow rubrics that allow for addressing new innovations and formats of teaching. These ideas have been field tested for six years with successful results. You will get customizable templates that have already been field tested and refined for moving from individual to group performance and organizational effectiveness and leadership development practice. We will discuss course organization, nature of learning activities, approaches to fostering student engagement and interaction, individual and group assignments, assessment and learning outcomes, "look and feel" of interface design, and evaluation of course effectiveness.

Our intention is that you use this as a practical guidebook and realize we are devoted to exploring the underlying dynamics of online teaching methods and their design. Our desire is to empower participants to create and teach courses that act as catalysts for rich and dynamic collaborative learning environments. It will be fun, inspirational, instructive, and provocative. It is action orientated and will provide a platform for guiding the existing skills that instructors already have in course writing and planning to a new level. Our hope is that participants will gain a fresh perspective about developing online courses for virtually any discipline and will be encouraged to deliver information through online learning environments.

In case you are wondering, What have I gotten myself into? let us give some background. For the past decade, Pepperdine University has been working with groups of students in education and the corporate world who are interested in entering the online learning arena or who are interested in improving the effectiveness of their existing online learning program. We know what we are doing well. We are good at what we do. We have a clear vision. We make improvements every year. The model that we present in the pages that follow will provide examples from experienced online instructors with the goal of preparing others to design and teach effectively in collaborative Web-based environments. We are experienced facilitators of online learning programs who understand the needs of faculty and learners, and we have developed an effective model leading to successful course outcomes.

We have created timesaving curriculum templates, resources, and research expertise, which will be useful in this proposed line of course development. As shown in figure A, Pepperdine's educational-technology

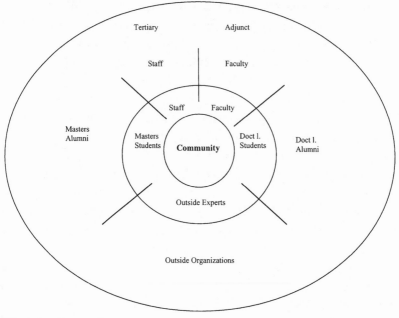

Figure A. *Community*

programs continue to combine the best of virtual and vertical learning. This illustration depicts the rich relationships engendered by Pepperdine's community approach. Community formation, support, and sustainability will also be explored. We will show that the benefits of integrating technology into your curriculum are great and can be done using the foundations of educational practice that are already familiar. We will show that e-learning is a more efficient way to learn when taught using this model. Based on the research collected over the past four years, over two hundred, or 92 percent, of students who took their course work online in our community model valued their education through the online program and successfully graduated.

Intended benefits from this reference guide include increased value to students, thereby leading to improved completion and recruitment and an increase of visibility for the program you teach in. Curriculum templates and documents will be included for dissemination at design meetings. Other deliverables include an easy-to-personalize and customize, detailed description of a developing model for integrating collaborative learning in community-based environments; a conceptual framework for the model based on relevant educational research; a collection and categorization of professional development materials in the form of a curriculum document and resource guide; a collection of developed evaluation tools; and rubrics that outline aspects of its evaluation. Upon completion of designing and teaching a course or doing faculty training with this model, you will be ready to report about what practitioners are actually doing and bring that information to your faculty with original content and examples.

The purpose of this "how to" guide will be to present a detailed program-development model of how to create a mutually supportive learning environment utilizing the Web. In the following, we have outlined the requirements for successfully designing and teaching a course while integrating Web-based technologies. When appropriate, a template is provided for guidance and clarity. Examples will be included that not only describe what participants perceive as enabling aspects of the support system, but also ways in which educators can enhance program development by learning from other pioneers in this area. This introduction should provide the reader with a context for interpreting the remaining chapters of this book. Each chapter explains a particular idea about designing and teaching online. In each chapter we will provide helpful outside resources and Web links to supplement, extend, or enrich the design materials to make this transition easier for you. A glossary for quick reference is available when clarification is needed. The bibliography lists references used in the handbook plus other related publications.

Because many teachers have unique requirements, the starting points, sequences, and tools selected will be as varied as the individual. We hope this will help you explore your imaginative possibilities for designing and facilitating online learning environments beyond the "givens" that exist in your workplace — standards, realistic time and resource constraints, and student achievement levels and interests.

Much of this model and these examples would be equally valuable when used in face-to-face classrooms. We recognize that good Web learning emulates good non-Web learning, but the literature seldom moves the conversation to the question, What things need to be emulated? We hope you enjoy our hands-on field guide for creating a great online course. We focus on the following question, What good learning design practices are found in effective Web-based programs?

CHAPTER 1

The Constructivist Approach to Online Learning with Technology

Education is the acquisition of the art of the utilization of knowledge. This is an art very difficult to impart. We must beware of what I will call "inert ideas" that is to say, ideas that are merely received into the mind without being utilized or tested or thrown into fresh combinations

—Whitehead

Constructivist theory draws from a variety of psychological and philosophical perspectives, including those of Piaget, Papert, Vygotsky, Bruner, and Dewey. The basis of constructivist theory is the idea that knowledge does not exist outside of the learner. Learners actively construct knowledge as they attempt to make sense of their experiences. The learners attempt to derive meaning from subject matter, and from this, are able to construct knowledge, forming mental structures, models, or schemas. They scaffold new knowledge into existing knowledge, thus connecting what they have learned with what they know.

CONSTRUCTIVIST LEARNING ENVIRONMENTS AND NEW TECHNOLOGIES

Lessons for the design of online learning environments demonstrate that students are likely to prefer visual representation and chunking of course content. We chunk content information into meaningful groups that are smaller and separated by headings. In these Web-enabled environments this reduces the cognitive load and therefore students can render more

1

obvious associations that might be hard to notice, or it can provide external memory to reduce the cognitive load. Students can notice patterns, desirable sub goals, or procedure chunks and identify in a discussion why one action is selected over another. Students cannot only reflect on and state their positions on an issue but can also compare their positions to those of their peers. They are able to observe and reflect on the decision process behind their peers' or instructors' choice of action. This keeps the cognitive (information) load bearable, because it's real time in a "learning by doing" discussion activity. This is designed to find ways for students to look at speaker, peer, or instructor choices and to see what choices had to be made, why they were made, and what the overall goal structure for peer and/or instructor performances might be. This is an important point; the reduction of the cognitive load on engaged students is important because it allows them to attend to constructing meaning and creating their own understanding of big ideas. The technology tools that allow large concepts to be mapped and symbolized, along with the ongoing recording of what has gone before, reduce the cognitive load by relieving the pressure of needing to remember details and histories. This seems especially important for the student, new to a community, who has had limited opportunities to incorporate understanding of complex ideas or utilize details enough that they become second nature.

In addition, the recording capabilities of the communication tools cut down on cognitive overload because these environments can act as external memories that keep the information most useful to productive activity readily available and can "replay" the past activity.

Examples of how this might happen can be seen with the use of distributed collaborators in dialogue, co-writing, imaging, simulations, and learning objects. Opportunities exist to interact with content, resources, experts, real-time data, and learning communities beyond the classroom walls. Learners can have access to, and can afford, the foremost authorities and the best advice on a topic. We have found in our practices that the learning that most students achieve during this process goes beyond the boundaries of what they are taught—far beyond what is solely the intent of the teacher. We see this repeatedly in our online teaching because individuals create meaning for themselves in their learning. Learning is a continual construction project.

As the learner encounters new experiences and particularly those that do not fit already into the realm of what is familiar, the learner revises his or her mental model to "accommodate" the new experiences. Vygotsky and his followers stress that this active construction of meaning occurs in a social context, where thought and language are actively verbal.

The learner negotiates meaning and tests understandings with teachers, mentors, or people who they perceive to be more knowledgeable peers. Learning, in this environment, is a social activity. In figure 1.1, adapted from Etienne Wenger's (1998) book *Communities of Practice*, the diagram illustrates a conceptual perspective of learning in relation to the situated learning theory. This design is not a replacement for other learning theories; instead, the focus of attention is on learning through social interaction. We encourage teachers to maximize opportunities for students to negotiate meanings in social contexts—to communicate and test understanding with and against that of others in an environment that is familiar and safe for the learner. This can be within their social environment, the course environment, and Web-based communities. It can also be cross-cultural when suitable. Regardless of the social environment, the long-term goal for the student is to become an active learner and to develop

Figure 1.1. *Components of Social Learning Theory*

enduring understandings of the subject matter. They will want to transfer their learning to the workplace and new situations. This process creates a community of learners who in this environment are able to engage in a process of collaborative inquiry that provides opportunities to see differences in what is noticed and understood as students from different workplaces explore the same general situations from their particular points of view. Reinforcing the theory of collaboration, we model that "learning and developing takes place within each learner, but it is also grounded to learning as a collective." (Putney and Wink, 2002, 121) We need to provide opportunities to build on, or challenge, students' understandings and preconceptions in order to transform or expand them. Working with these understandings helps learners of all ages, and a community model fosters this constructivist approach to learning. During the last decade, technology has become a powerful tool for effective communication. We have greatly advanced how people learn with these communication tools in "anchored collaboration,"—collaboration that is structured around a main topic or issue—through discussions online. While conceptual frameworks help for a better and faster transfer to new situations, the metacognitive approach, first modeled by the instructor, allows students to practice and discuss strategies as they learn to use them.

The beauty of the non-linear Web learning experience is that we can search for knowledge in an order that makes sense to each of us, the individual learner. We can also see how others have made sense of things without having to adopt that strategy as our way of organizing our learning. New understandings of how people learn suggest that learning is maximized in rich and complex learning environments that offer multiple opportunities for hands-on learning, quality dialogue with others, making connections across disciplines, and various forms of expression. Online learning is an attempt to teach general problem solving and thinking skills/inquiry procedures, which require well-organized knowledge that is accessible in appropriate contexts. The Web can provide this through communal databases that have text, "notes," and graphic capabilities. The student can create "interconnected pathways" via search engines and links, multiple windows of resources, and interfaces that allow students to co-build knowledge—connected knowledge.

Online Learning is an Epiphany by Design

Investigating the instructive strategies of a program that promotes dialogue and collective intellect in a community model will benefit faculty in designing Web-based courses by helping to develop and apply technologies that improve teaching, course design, and management. There are many advantages for students to choose an online course. The following are just a few of the reasons.

Learning at Their Own Pace

Online learning has many advantages for students. Most learners like the online environment because they can learn at their own pace and at times that are most convenient for them. Students who have more background knowledge in a subject can move through material more quickly. If they have to set aside class for a period of time, they can easily return to the content and review what they have missed. Many students learn faster online because they can skip through information they already know and focus on learning new and unique content. This can be compared to listening to music on CD versus a cassette tape—in a well designed course it is much easier to search and skip forward or go back and repeat without rewinding or losing your place in a book.

Learning When Most Convenient

Many students today are active in their communities, have family responsibilities, and work full- or part-time. The flexibility of online learning allows them to pursue their educational goals at the same time. Students can study at their optimal learning time of day or night, and increased engagement is the result. Many of us would not be at school during the hours we choose to be online. This allows more privacy for some instructional situations as well. Class facilitation in cyberspace has the potential to occur around the clock. The Internet never stops, and as a result, the class will be thinking and talking essentially at any given time on any given day. You will, of course, have specific class time where the group will meet to connect specific ideas. Outside of this time, students can keep up the flow of conversation by following asynchronous discussions.

Learning Suited to Their Learning Styles

Students learn in many different ways. Content can be created that delivers materials in ways that take advantage of these different learning styles. When students are presented with content and resources in their preferred learning style, they learn better. The online tools exist today to provide this level of support for learning, including text, audio, self-testing, Internet links, and dialogue with instructor and peers. Our students often say that online learning addresses their visual and auditory learning styles by not only allowing them to "hear" their peer's discussion in synchronous class sessions but also having the re-enforcement of reading it simultaneous to hearing it. Technology helps the teacher prepare and display problems that the class works on collaboratively. This in turn allows students to collaborate, question, and construct meaning on their own, while at the same time being supported by a community.

Learning Through Increased Access to Information

Online, the information can be as in-depth as one wants. The student can have access to the world's finest libraries, current news events, academic journals, and up-to-date research. Students have the opportunity to engage in dialogue with leading experts in their discipline through email, discussion boards, and chat sessions. They are able to communicate and collaborate with other learners across national boundaries, helping them to develop a global perspective on issues. The use of Web-based course development tools allows students to get enhanced learning experiences that they might not otherwise get in a more conventional educational setting.

Learning through Increased Choices

Online learning allows a variety of choices for the learner. Students can determine which activities and projects they would like to work on as they strive to meet course objectives. The multitude of choices available on the Internet allow "page turning" Web sites to be transformed into a smorgasbord of interactive learning opportunities suited to the individual student's learning style. Instructors have access to ready-made learning objects and simulation that can be used to enhance the traditional "lecture" delivery mode of information and demonstrate how the lecture is just one of many tools that can be used by teachers in order to facilitate the learning of their students.

Learning through Purposeful Customization

Often, online courses fail to utilize the rich opportunities that exist in this unique environment. To some extent, even with multimedia and human interaction, students end up sitting in front of a computer "turning the page" rather than being engaged in the learning experience. How much can we vary online activities? Even if we use words such as "create," "list," and "discuss," we are still saying, "sit in front of the computer, look at the screen, and type." New strategies in effective development and delivery of online courses are necessary for the successful transfer of knowledge utilizing the Internet. From an instructor's perspective, the Internet can create the impetus for the online environment to essentially transport him or her into the learner's workspace, where relevant hands-on experiences can be crafted. At Pepperdine, we address this issue by involving students in projects carried out in their workplace and communities, both online and face to face, so that eventually there will be much less "online" in online learning. Purposeful customization is dependent on instructors that have learned how to adapt their content and teaching styles for an online environment.

Less "online" in online learning has enough rough edges that it is interesting but hard to swallow. An anecdotal illustration may help. Learners in our program break the barriers of school walls with electronic networking. Connecting with the larger professional community, working on meaningful projects in collaboration with peers and faculty, and reflecting on those experiences all enable students to construct deeper understandings of subject matter than in traditional settings. Students learn how technology can support innovative ideas in learning environments—constructivism, dialogue, alternate assessment, collaboration, and community—by experiencing them directly, as learners in real and virtual classrooms. The program also prepares students to lead others, develop colleagues, manage resources, make technology decisions, and secure project funding. Students work with multimedia, groupware, and Net-based applications and hardware and become fully engaged in an electronic learning community. A frequently held view of online learning is one that expects that the interaction exists between the student and online data sets. In fact, online learning really becomes collaboration with a much larger community, with a wider range of expertise. After all, the Web is really all about community and the sharing of information (www.fastcompany.com/online/56/internet101. html). Finding and collaborating with experts and near peers all facilitate experience that can be far more social then brick-and-mortar classrooms.

Learning through Interaction

Humans learn by interacting, asking questions, responding to others, replying to the instructor. Interaction prompts more interaction, and this in turn stimulates ideas, reactions, challenges, and, possibly, differences. Participants have questions, perspectives, and ideas that are valuable. When other learners are engaged in answering questions, they explore and examine concepts more, think more, and share more. Classes where participants have no interaction with their classmates are similar to correspondence courses.

SOCIAL NATURE OF LEARNING

"A mind is a fire to be kindled, not a vessel to be filled"

—Plutarch

The Institute for Research on Learning has formulated several principles about the social nature of learning, many of which relate to communities (Beer, 2000). These include the social nature of learning, learning as an act of membership, knowledge as being dependent on engagement, and exclusion from participation resulting in the failure to learn. Many instructors used to think of learners as empty vessels, but no longer.

Student Expectations

The expectations of today's students are changing from what we have become accustomed to in the past. Exposure to entertainment, the tools they use to communicate, their mobility, and the Internet are all factors in students wanting more project-based learning. Students want more control because they have it in other areas of their lives. They want education that better serves their needs and interests. They learn best when the topic is of immediate value. Facilitators can tap into this diversity of experience and idea sharing to enhance the course and learning for all.

Effective online learning allows the student to "work smarter." In our course model, the student is empowered to work smarter because the emphasis is on discovery learning and problem solving through project-based learning activities. Students use a plethora of online resources to perform research, communicate with experts via the Internet, access real-time data. They develop graphic design, communications, and presentation skills that will enhance their classroom and workplace performance. Teachers can also work smarter with their students by using many of the "real time" tools that allow for chat-like sessions (including voice with the right bandwidth), which also allows teachers and their students to share the computer desktops. This means a teacher can see what the students are doing on their computers if they choose to share. Many instructors use this in a lab setting. Students can sit back and watch the instructor demo without having to squint at the overhead in front of class in a face-to-face session. This will also be a good way for instructors to be with their students and help them, for example, troubleshoot concerns and debug programs, in a 100 percent online class. To best utilize this tool, an instructor could set up a lab time where students can connect to the tools provided by the instructor and be able to ask questions and show the instructor the problems they are having with their project or code so that the instructor and student can step through and debug together during the session.

Methodologies for Delivering Constructivist Education

We will explore instructive methodologies for teachers to support the design and delivery of their knowledge of a particular subject matter. These technologies are not just rich sources of information but, more importantly, are extensions of human capabilities and contexts for social interactions to support and expand learning. Learning research needs to be constantly considered as these Web tools develop and as we integrate them into educational environments. This complex, activity-rich learning environment arouses interest and curiosity in the learner and offers multiple contexts to make meaning.

Instruction and assessment must respond to the learners' natural inclination and/or desire to see patterns, make connections, create ideas, and express themselves. When possible, learning and instruction needs to be connected to what the learner already knows. The learners need to see how this knowledge may apply to their lives for potential application in new situations. Learners must also be given the opportunity to demonstrate their learning in authentic contexts for workplace readiness. Without knowledge, context, and real-life application, many students would not start making changes in their workplace until after the course or program is over. Learners need authentic performance-based instruction and assessment. To create this we use a backward design. We look at what we ask the learners to know and be able to do and what constitutes evidence of its attainment, and then we begin course development with the end in mind.

Technologies help us capture interactions between students and the instructor as they engage in teaching and learning. All online-delivery platforms have their positives and negatives, so no one system is the best. However, in our current online program in educational technology at Pepperdine University, we focus our energies on developing curriculum, which utilizes Internet tools to deliver the program in a situated context (community-based model). This model will be featured as an example of an effective collaborative learning environment being executed on the Internet. The goal is to move the learner toward important understandings, knowledge, or skills, so one must carefully think about the key elements one is striving for in design. Next, we will explore and examine possible instruction, activities, and assignments that would be appropriate for meeting the criteria. We have created an authentic environment by real-world application of course work. Now we will show you how to do the same in your own collaborative environment. You will see more anecdotal descriptions and illustrations of what you can make to help visualize your new future online classroom in the following chapters.

CHAPTER 2

Effective Planning and Design
for Online Teaching

Socrates noted that a teacher is only a midwife to students, who must carry out the labor of learning themselves. There is no learning unless the student is the worker. The student learns by listening, by writing, by arguing, by imagining, by building, by drawing, by experiencing.

The online arena creates opportunities for the integration of technology to facilitate student learning. Successful use of these technologies depends, in large part, on the planning, preparation and implementation by the instructor.

The rapid pace of technological change and its requirements for life-long learning, the complexity of our society and its escalating challenges and finite resources, and the need to prepare an increasingly diverse student population to live productively and harmoniously requires academia to discover new ways of addressing the discovery, dissemination, and implementation of knowledge. Education can no longer be defined by static guidelines but rather by growing, changing, and evolving new sets of opportunities, projects, technology, and people. Education is the soul of the new information-systems society. It serves as an enabler for students to synthesize knowledge and to create, perform, and encourage, their passion for learning.

Allowing technology to be a platform—a conceptually open environment—where students can gain knowledge in multiple formats gives students the opportunity to discover relationships between concepts and how they relate to real-life events. By demystifying technology for teachers and students and providing the tools needed to integrate technology, we are giving them more control over their future. In socio-cultural theory, learning is a matter of enculturation; your identity evolves through access to knowledge or expertise in use around you and through interaction with objects and people engaging with you in practical work (Lave and Wenger, 1991; Wenger, 1998). For example, by developing models that utilize the power of the Internet, we equip instructors with an abundant supply of quality curriculum options that integrates technology and allows teachers to choose from a wealth of instructional materials to customize their teaching.

WEB-ENHANCED TEACHING

There is no question that the Internet is changing how we learn. The potential of the Internet as a learning tool is just beginning to be tapped into as a teaching resource.

Why Use the Web?

The fundamental value proposition for teaching and learning on the Web is human performance achievement. Productivity improvements and academic results have been demonstrated with technology-mediated instruction (Kulik and Kulik, 1986; Kulik, Kulik, and Bangert-Drowns 1990), and performance improvement is the goal we are after. The Web helps instructors deliver on the value proposition. Today, students are looking for "me learning" in e-learning. It is not necessarily about the tool or software used in the process; it is about the ability we have in practice to offer more personalization for the learner. So, how can we leverage and appreciate the potential of new technologies and match them up with students' learning styles? Technology can augment and solve a large variety of parameters. It far surpasses the human capability to do that. With the Internet revolution, we can move toward personalization of learning with a large scale of information. Web-based tools allow instructors to customize content, tools, time, and context, among other aspects of the learning environment.

The Web also helps teachers by allowing students to explore, examine, and participate in developing job skills for projects in the workplace. This is because almost all of our work today is project-based. So, we need instructional use, creation, and manipulation of learning objects, including many pre-made components. A learning object is any digital resource that can be reused to support learning. This definition includes anything that can be delivered across the network on demand, be it large or small (Wiley, 2000, 7). The role of the instructor is to guide students around the content and engage them in constructive and creative problem-solving strategies.

On individualized learning, Bloom found that the average student who is tutored scores better than 98 percent of classroom students. Teacher and Web communities can purposefully support that. We have to help students make competent decisions, and this is why collaboration is an important part of the process. The instructor starts the discussion and provides direction and facilitation, making sure that the students are thinking and talking about the important aspects of the content. This collaborative design is not "cookie cutter" or canned; rather, it is assembled by the instructor with active participation from the student.

Technology as a Tool

Online learning uses technology to extend good teaching, not to replace good teachers. The technology is embedded into other proven methods of instruction. During the last decade, technology has emerged as a powerful tool for effective communication. We have greatly advanced how people learn with these communication tools. The use of technology assists in creating a flexible environment and making those adaptations fluid for the learner. Much of our theoretical foundation is based on learner-centered and constructivist approaches. When creating your online course, many factors need to be considered: the type of students enrolled, the technology available to your students, and whether the course is going to be offered fully online or as a hybrid Web-enhanced course. Students have varied backgrounds that we, as designers and teachers, can adapt to via flexible access.

The Pepperdine model clearly promotes the value of a community of learners. The need to remove impediments to collaboration and cooperation has never been greater. I view my role as that of a learning-environment architect, working to remove the barriers that separate students and knowledge and allow them to pursue meaningful lives that embrace theories of lifelong learning. Students have incredible networking energy. We encourage learners to share ideas with each other and then with the instructor. In your community, you may have people from all fields of expertise. As mentors in his or her individual fields, each one will become a resource for the rest of the community. They will teach one another, and, in turn, the group becomes greater than the sum of its parts. Your community essentially takes the form of a family or cohort. This family is a place that constructively gives support, guidance, feedback, and friendship to the other members. You, as the leader, hold the umbrella of big ideas that link to the larger concepts. In the end, you will see evidence of learning among your community. This process of creating your community enables a new level of communication to be reached via the strategy and tools being used by both the instructor and the student.

Unlike a traditional classroom that moves in lockstep to a well-defined syllabus (that is measured by minutes and hours), learning is sometimes difficult to observe—even by those involved in the collaborative effort. The advantage to a collaborative community is the direct involvement that is required for the acquisition of knowledge. One student observed, "Ideas are out there for all to see and comment on, which lends itself to our examining of what we are doing and learning. . . . We get to see the big picture." There is a shift from an emphasis on the individual learner to one of a shared community and collaborative meaning making. Rather than being subjected to a directive, teacher-driven approach, the students are being guided in how to accomplish something that they have chosen. Students are in control of their own learning, which makes the learning more meaningful. Giving students choices in layers of communication for synchronous communication (e.g., chat, videoconferencing, instant messaging, and telephone conversations), allows them a greater amount of ownership and confidence when working in collaboration with other students. Their vested interest in the outcome is an important factor when it comes to motivation because the learning is no longer an external manifestation that is held inside a textbook; rather the learning is internal and depends on their decisions of what to include or exclude. Students rely on one another for the completing of group assignments and moving group synchronous and asynchronous discussion along in a constructive manner.

As we discuss communities of practice, we intend to encourage, model, and support instructional sharing. Knowledge is constructed as a result of the community discourse reflected in shared understanding, and it is especially evident in co-production, whether as idea, theory, publication, or project. This process of creating your community enables a new level of communication to be reached because of the strategy and tools being used by both the instructor and the student.

Pepperdine University Online Master's in Educational Technology program advocates a situated constructivist learning structure. In a constructivist technique, users select content from multiple paths of content and learning activities—thus creating their own sequence of instruction. Like K. Patricia Cross, a professor of education at the University of California, Berkeley, we found that learning is not so much an additive process, with new learning simply piling up on top of existing knowledge, as it is an active, dynamic process in which the connections are constantly changing and the structure reformatted. The instructor assists and scaffolds the sharing and responses and gives suggestions to guide and intellectually support the student in this co-production or project.

Online, people from different disciplines, interests, and levels of experience can come together to explore their creative processes. Whether you are a writer, a corporate trainer, a teacher, or an artist, we can help you, the instructor, discover and nurture the particular style of expression that occurs in the online environment. Constructivist-inspired activities and collaborative online learning encourage creativity, analogies, and story telling related to content from the learner's prior experiences. One actually *does* what the readings for the course talk about—applying those theories in real-life settings makes students feel more in tune with theories, bringing the experience full circle for both the learner and the instructor. Situated constructivist learning allows students to process information according to its practical applications in authentic contexts. Students have access to and utilize a variety of technological tools, people, resources, activities, interaction, and learning strategies through which to demonstrate their knowledge. They are engaged in contextual learning by utilizing multi-sensory approaches. Thoughtful implementation of this learning model has proven effective and successful in many online courses. The end product is an expanded perception of fact and theory, innovative problem solving, and ways of looking at one's life and work as exciting and transformative.

TRANSLATING CONTENT TO WEB-BASED ENVIRONMENTS

Where Do I Start?

You will need to work toward developing a realistic strategic pedagogical model for your specific online learning environment. Figure 2.1 illustrates the key factors that influence the design of online course material and shows how the different layers of design relate to one another.

Teaching strategies and templates have sustainability—tools do not; tools change. You will need to give to the learner support tools and options. The interactive Web tool is not as important as what the learner does with it. We are interested in the meaningful use of tools, but re-

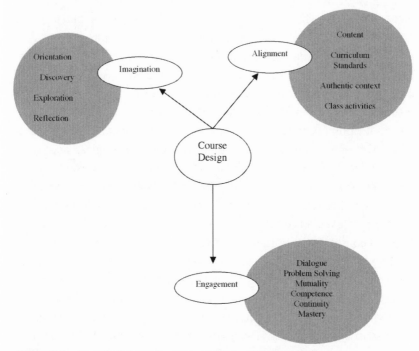

Figure 2.1.   *Sample Schematic of Course Design (Wenger, 1998)*

member to be open to change; like a new tool, it will offer potential to expand the experience to new levels.

Through online interaction, students learn the value of dialogue, conversation, and personal relationships built within a community environment. They learn that the dialogue among the group is equally important as the technology being used, theories learned, or processes implemented. Instructors must design effective online learning experiences so students spend time talking to one another about what they learned. There is a metacognitive aspect to the students' conversations as well. Student discussion of the "how" impacts the quality and quantity of the "what." This means giving students opportunities to respond to the material you presented around the topic. While technology may be helpful in the workplace and/or classroom, it is more valuable in the way it helps people to collaborate and communicate in their immediate community.

Planning and Organizing

When you assign projects, you also have to figure out the amount of time it takes to review each project, post feedback, assess learning for each student, and evaluate his or her progress through the course. Instructors, who do not know their students, will find it difficult to evaluate the students' progress or their ability to assimilate the information. Working backward from the concept of community, it is critical to incorporate activities that will allow you to get to know your students, and encourage them to know one another, early in the course. In the list below, we are able to show many different ideas for interactive communication that will stimulate activity based interaction:

Concept mapping	Web Partners/ Peer Editing	Character Dialogue
Timelines	Demonstrations	Personal Vignettes
Taxonomies	Values Clarification	Mnemonics
Summary writing	Simulations	Jigsaw Grouping
Jeopardy style quizzes	Case Studies	Rank/Report

Fireside Chats	Role Plays	"In a Fishbowl"
Internet Searches	Small Group Projects	Incomplete Statements
Student Portfolios	Panel Discussions	Theatrics
Conference-style Presentations	Brainstorm Sessions	Critical Incidents
Alter Ego	Buzz Sessions	Student/Guest Interviews
Flow Charts	Structured Overviews	Leading Questions
Discussion Boards	Chat Rooms	Learning Circles
Guest Speakers	Content Chunking	Skits
Learning Objects	Quotes	Journals

As the instructor, you will need to be organized, provide clear directions, and set clear guidelines, expectations, and policies on blended learning. When you are designing your course, build in redundancy to help students understand what is expected of them.

Steps for Creating Your Online Course

1. Select learning goals, outcomes, competencies, and issue importance, in the subject you teach or area of study.
2. Select readings—they need to be focused and purposeful.
   a. What kind of information will students find useful?
   b. How can this benefit them?
3. Develop and post your course syllabus. The instructor's syllabus and discussion postings need to give students the road map to what the important concepts are for the course. Think, how can you embed Web-based tools? Explore and examine what tools are available to you. (See appendix C for tools author recommends.)
4. Create lessons, units, or modules (sometimes chapters in books can be module topics). Each unit focuses around a different topic and/or competency. Create five to ten units based on the length of the course and content.
5. Identify what would be a useful application of the desired knowledge for students.

6. Answer, does the learner have to "produce" anything? What would be the most effective way for students to demonstrate the information they have learned?
7. Provide forum for interaction. Create discussion questions for activities. Elicit performance. Create activities to practice new skills or behaviors and to apply understanding and improve retention.
8. Provide learning guidance with locally relevant examples, case studies, and graphical representations.
9. Plan for assessment. Design effective and meaningful assessments in which the students take the concepts and theories they have been learning and investigating and apply them to open ended questions or project based assignments that are authentic and can be applied to real world situations.

Course Readiness Guidelines

The following are basic course readiness guidelines that can be applied to various online courses. As an instructor, your answers to the following questions should be positive before attempting to establish an online course.

These guidelines are good, but in many colleges, the instructor *is* the technical support person and the one responsible for orienting the students to online learning. So ideally, we realize some of this support will need to be built in by future administrative leadership as these techniques and student enrollment evolve.

Student Support

- Do students receive email and mail confirmations and passwords after registering with orientation information about taking a course online?
- Do students take a face-to-face or online orientation to online learning?
- Is there technical support for your students?
- Is there a plan for getting in touch with students if the server goes down (e.g., a phone tree or instant messaging)?

Content Development

- Is there a textbook or set of readings for your course?
- Is there appropriate instructional media and resources in mixed modes of online, CD-ROM, video, audio, print-based, and re-source kits, other than the online copy for your course?
- Do you provide rich associations for key concepts you teach (e.g., show where things occur in real databases, links to experts, and real-life applications) so that learning is organized around life application?
- Do you make use of spatial metaphors as mental models to help students become accustomed to the online structure of your course?
- Is the course divided into modules or units?
- Is the online text/copy chunked in "bite size," meaningful units?
- Is the online copy supplemental to the readings (answer "yes") or the primary source of readings (answer "no") for the course?
- Have you secured copyright permission for any non-original material (not covered by the Fair Use Guidelines) used in the course?
- Do you have conceptual discussion questions and starter comments related to the desired outcomes for online discussion for each of your units?
- Do you have guidelines and rules for online discussion for your students to encourage them to share experiences and refine ideas?
- Do you have guidelines or a framework for peer projects?
- Do you have formative and summative assessment strategies in place?
- Do you have a final exam, group project, individual project, or other course-evaluation activities determined?
- Do you have grading criteria determined for your course for assignment timeliness and content?
- Are online discussion comments a part of the student's grade?
- Will all discussion related to the course and course content be conducted in the discussion areas (e.g., threaded discussions, listserv, real-time chat, instant messaging)?

Technical Issues

- Do you have a technical person or support staff for your course?
- Have you and your campus technical support staff met to discuss technical requirements for your course?

- Do you have a phone number to contact your tech support after hours?
- Have you identified teaching tools?
- Are you trained and comfortable with all the functions of your online classroom tools?
- Have you dealt with Web accessibility for any students with disabilities?
- Have you thought about presence redundancy? Have your materials up in two places so if one server goes down it is still available.

Course Management

- Do you have a Welcome page with announcements, upcoming activities, timely bulletins about changes and updates to the course, and instructions and notes for each section?
- Have you set aside the time and created a way to "break the ice" and help students get acquainted online during the first few weeks of the course?
- Will you be logging into your online course once a day during the course?
- Do you have a policy to limit email to the instructor to personal and individual student issues?
- Do you have one or more physical settings where you can teach online without distraction and interruption?
- Do you have a method of gaining student feedback about your course online (e.g., a form and/or hard copy to mail out)?

Once you have the structure in place, it is time to deal with the transfer of course content from a traditional face-to-face model to an online Web-based environment. The following sections will address the questions raised in the above guidelines and deal with the details on how to run your online course more effectively to enhance student achievement and understanding.

Creating a Web Site for Your Course

Once you have created your syllabus and decided on your competencies and the topics you will cover, it is time to create your Web site.

This Web site is important to students because it will be a place that they go to for information about meeting times, assignment topics, guidelines, resources, and due dates—a place of consistency. Instructor pages need to be well designed and contain consistent design elements because flaws and non-intuitive variations create learner frustration.

Content needs to be chunked and organized meaningfully and demonstrated with rich media, visual metaphors, and/or mental models. Screen objects need logical order placement. Be consistent in visual cues, and use media choices that add clarity and are consistent with objectives. However, limit peripheral images. Use animation, background noise, and audio sparingly. Written text on the Internet needs to be "chunked"; that is, it needs to be brief, one to two paragraphs per concept. Use bulleted, boldfaced, highlighted, and/or underlined text where necessary to draw out the key points. Research shows that people scan Web pages on the Internet; they do not read (Nielsen, www .useit.com/alertbox/20000514.html).

When placing text on the screen, try not to have long sentences that run the full width of the screen. Instead, use only half the screen by creating large left and right margins. This will make the text easier to read, and important points will be recognized more easily. We do this so students do not get into the "butterfly defect," sampling multiple resources or sites but none of them in-depth or with purposeful reflection (Salomon, 1998).

The syllabus you post on your Web site is extremely important to students and needs to be clear and informative. You need to establish curricular priorities and develop a content outline. This will help in the creation of learning objectives for your course. You will need to inform learners of these objectives early on in the program so they will know what is to come. By knowing the objectives from the beginning of a course, everyone understands what is expected of them. Students are aware of what is required in terms of participation and level of work submitted as assessment, and you, the instructor, will be able to anticipate the needs and expectations of the students.

Menus on your Web site should, ideally, contain no more than seven items. Submenus need titles that show selected options from the previous menus, and the order of placement of menu items should match the structure of tasks. If no sequence is associated with menu items, place the most frequently used at the top and less frequently used at the bottom. Buttons need to be easily found and grouped based on a particular function. Be sure that each button has a function and is not obsolete. Any screen messages that you have on your site need to be friendly, polite, and informative. Text needs to be consistent throughout the site, including any special headings, fonts, and size changes. Consistency is the key to a functional and visually appealing Web site that is easy to navigate and leaves viewers with an overall feeling of being successful in obtaining the information they seek.

Include on your Web site some short- and long-term project or assignment options in multiple formats that allow the students some flexibility and choice. A range of resources, reading options, audio and visual clips, animation, music, and video should also be included if appropriate. There should also be access to exemplary student projects and assignments from past classes for current students to view and investigate. Students should also be encouraged to initiate additional resources that you could include on your site, such as guest speakers and other issues. One last thing to remember to include is a "mail to" link or a way for students to be able to contact you through your Web site.

When creating Web materials for your course, you should do an analysis of your design before the beginning and again at the end to ensure that everything needed has been included in the materials. Any surveys or questionnaires that you create should have specific questions whose results are then reviewed and summarized somewhere on your site. To determine the effectiveness of your course and the materials you have created, you can gather feedback via the following methods:

1. Direct observation—observe the learner using course.
2. Indirect observations such as help desk, evaluations, and error rates.
3. Focus groups—pose questions to a group of students. Data comes from direct answers and conversations among focus-group participants.
4. Offer a feedback option on your site for outside observers' feedback.

An emphasis should be placed on the following skills: problem solving skill building, English skill building, and computer skill building, as well as the other course concepts.

A design process that we use involves creating cycles of projects, dealing with individual and group dynamics, recognizing what is effective and what is not, and coming up with the content to be learned, while allowing students to create the medium for how they will learn and experience it and all actions that should be taken. Each of these requires research, action, and reflection both on the part of the students and the instructor.

Example: Course Content and Study Framework

A. Introduce assignment information.
B. Conduct "KWL," or pre-test, for self-assessment.

   For example, when I use "KWL," I take one of those large virtual whiteboards or pieces of paper and divide it into three columns. Under "K" we list what we know (pre-assessment), under "W" we list what they think they will learn or want to learn (goal setting), and under "L" we leave a blank space. We leave the blank space up throughout the unit and the students have me fill in things in the "L" column as they encounter and/or understand them. So for us, "L" stands for what we learned. The students love it when I put something in that column that they taught me, too.

C. Read the chapter and learn vocabulary (really important to learn vocabulary).
D. View media on their own time or with class in real time discussions.
E. Visit Web sites—post reactions on asynchronous tool (often called Discussion Area, example: a class newsgroup).
F. Do task (e.g., case study)—post solutions on personal Web page and/or in asynchronous tool (often called Discussion Area, for example, a class newsgroup).
G. Ask reflective questions or give review test for self-assessment.

A "learner packet," or a study guide for how to be successful in this course (study guide), might be helpful for students to focus on key concepts. Some programs and instructors print and distribute a learner packet that contains much of the material that they make available in the online course. It may seem an unnecessary duplication, and most instructors are not very much in favor of the plan, as it might appear to lessen the students' commitment to going online. However, it has turned out to be popular with some students—perhaps because they feel secure in having the hard copy and because it can be used to quickly locate or review course content and can be read anywhere. Making the file available online in a printable document format is a good substitute. It is important when encouraging change not to eliminate too much where people feel comfortable. In encouraging the leaner to "join the cause" and participate in online learning, you are not dismissing the importance of printed material. You are just showing that there is more than one option. One of the biggest functionalities that students ask for is the ability to work offline, and while this is not always realistic, providing a learner packet as an overview of key information will assist in the flexibility and functionality of your course.

It is also helpful to provide tips on Internet note-taking using diagrams and charts that can be accessed from the instructor's Web site. Another benefit to an online course is that an easy to record audiocassette can be transcribed and posted to your Web site. It is important to remember that for optimal retention, you should chunk the audio in presentation as if it were text. Keep multimedia in reasonable chunks since available bandwidth is a consideration, especially when using streaming audio and video.

Contextual Considerations

Know how to take contextual considerations (e.g., instructional materials, student interests, needs, aptitudes, and community resources) into account in planning collaborative online instruction. This creates an effective bridge between curriculum goals and student experiences. The online learning environment gives students better access to additional learning resources when they need them and at the level they require.

Goals need to be written in a way that meet the needs of multiple learning styles. Visualize the students who will be taking your course, and anticipate their needs. Provide many alternatives in terms of resources—the readings, references to various authorities on the course focus, video, and audio. You want the students to find their special niche for learning. With Web resources and tools available for connecting and extending human capabilities, you have a variety of teaching methods to represent your material so that your students can learn in a number of different modes.

The way you present and facilitate your material makes the student want to enroll and stay in your class. Online course development gives you an opportunity to define and present your style. Emphasize discovery learning and problem solving through project-based learning activities where students use online resources to perform research, communicate with experts via the Internet and real-time data, and develop graphic-design and communications and presentation skills to enhance their classroom and/or workplace performance.

Enriched Opportunities

Activities should provide enriched opportunities to engage in interesting and productive demonstrations of knowledge. For example, have students read information on the topic and ask them to take notes to share with classmates. They can fill out a chart or diagram while watching a streamed video or take notes on an audio presentation. Ask the students to discuss their observations with a colleague and report back to the class with a summary of the conversation.

Purposeful projects and discussions need to be given on a regular basis in courses. High expectations yield high results. Frequent, formative assessment helps makes students' thinking visible to themselves, their peers, and the instructor. Interactive activities, games, hands-on projects, or tasks need a set time limit. Allow for some individual work time as well as group-work time (e.g., think, pair, and share activity).

Assessing Learning

Create learning assessments that encourage the use of the course content rather than just the knowledge of the course content. In chapter 5 we will go into detail about how to create authentic assessments of student learning. However, in planning your course, you can consider the following strategy. One option is an online course that pre-tests before each module. Based on the results, you could select complete module or custom presentation order. Some folks never do well on the pre-test, but it provides an introduction to the concepts that follow. After the modules have been presented, a post-test is administered. Students feel the pre-test primed the pump of explicit learning, and the module builds the tacit knowledge. The post-test confirms that they learned what they should have learned.

Submitting Assignments

As the instructor, you will have to decide how you would like students to submit their assignments to you. You should give clear and specific instructions so that everyone is aware of where to let others know their assignments are located so they may give feedback. Whatever you decide, it should be easy for the students to do and appropriate for the assignment. If the assignment is for students to discuss, then maybe it should be posted in the threaded discussion area so that comments can be made and a conversation initiated. If it is a final project, then maybe posting on the Web would be most appropriate. Some options for consideration are:

1. Text documents can be emailed as attachments. Instructors may specify the type of word-processing program that the students can use for ease of viewing.
2. Assignments may be typed into an email with no attachment.
3. Assignments may be typed into the class discussion area and posted.
4. Web-based documents may be published on the Web.
5. Documents may be printed to PDF files and posted on the Web or emailed to the instructor.
6. Projects can be transferred to a knowledge database.
7. Some systems allow for posting of all assignments into a folder.

Learning Objects

When instructors first gain access to instructional materials, they often carve up the materials into their essential parts and then reassemble these parts in ways that support their individual needs and goals. This suggests one reason why learning objects may provide instructional benefits. If instructors received instructional resources as individual components, the initial step of decomposition could be bypassed, potentially boosting the speed and effectiveness of instructional design for the Web. In building up the strength of a course through a component-based model, identifying objectives equates to the competencies one is trying to obtain. We assemble learning objects and content pieces around that.

The instructional object has great potential as a common building block for a diverse range of technology-based instructional products (Richards, 4). These can be pre-built and accelerate authoring tasks. The reusability goes up as granular size goes down. A learning object is not a single definable object; it is a multi-faceted technological teaching tool (Richards, 1) that is targeted to all students and all levels of ability. It creates a forward motion of knowledge transfer. A learning object allows for the learner to chunk pieces of information together to build a network of knowledge. Computers make possible a new form of narrative expression in which manipulatible technology objects are set in text.

Learning objects create a basic idea and put a familiar face on new instructional technology (Wiley, 2000, 15). A good learning object teaches a single concept or skill (Orrill, 2000, 3). The use of a learning object assists in creating communities that support the development of understanding on a number of levels. Learning objects allow for learning by doing. Activities are "scaffolded" so learners move from a place of little understanding to having a grasp on the concept at hand. Using learning objects in constructivist ways requires some rethinking of the objects and careful consideration of their use (Orrill, 2000, 4). Some examples include learning experiences that emerging technologies use to teach in the online environment and video case scenarios in related contexts to the content.

Learning Units as Learning Objects

A wonderful repository of peer-reviewed learning units can be found at the Merlot Project (www.merlot.org). Accomplished Web instructors and designers use these units and objects to establish a caring, stimulating, inclusive, and safe community for learning where students take intellectual risks and work independently and collaboratively.

Technology has provided the tools and the leverage to reshape learning environments. These "new" environments are based on a constructivist foundation, and they frequently revolve around project engagement on the part of the student. For teachers and trainers that are responsible for meeting knowledge and skill goals, the challenge of creating a new environment that addresses the curricular demands is a formidable one.

This section examines how Web-based learning environments that are project based can meet steep curricular goals. Instructors can integrate these models and emerging technologies to reshape environments in which they lead or participate. We have updated our knowledge and expanded our repertoire of strategies for shaping learning environments to plan and carry out interventions or modifications to utilize the Web more effectively.

Using learning objects, the instructor can construct a learning path that allows students to investigate new information in their own way. One can populate the path with different content and therefore maximize usability of the learning objects. Instructors can identify learning objects and build knowledge architecture on a personalized basis with projects that fulfill students' needs better.

Web Projects

Web projects are a natural choice for integrating across the curriculum and skill building. I am convinced that students really need to work with tools (concepts and ideas, as well as material tools) in order to understand them deeply and fully. I am indeed working with our new tools in discourse when we use them to shape our talks, share minds, and establish interpersonal relationships and joint understanding. However, the projects are designed to take work with the course tools a step further, into another context and/or activity, out there in the "real world." Figures 2.2 through 2.5 are examples of the case-study assignment where each student examines his or her practice while working toward reform in his or her workplace. The student can then learn concretely

EDC665 Case Study Analysis Final Project Part 1

Case Study Project Description
View the Evaluation Rubric Or the Sample Case Studies Assess the environment of your workplace for its effectiveness in utilization and support of technology.

This analysis should outline specific facts, problems, and solutions. You should consider the folowing questions:

1. What is the nature of the workplace? What kind of work is done there? Who is involved?
2. What tasks in your workplace are being addressed with technology presently and how effective is the application of technology in those tasks?
3. What are the inappropriate uses of technology in your workplace?
4. What level of support is present for technology use and what further support, if any, is required?
5. What improvements should be made?
6. Within reasonable resource limits, what tasks in your workplace should technology address in the future? As you report your analysis, refer to the readings and topics of this course, where applicable.

Recommended Format/Structure

Use APA format for citations and references. Address the questions above by structuring your analysis into these six sections:

1. Introduction and Purpose
2. Central Questions (This is the question you are asking, for example:

   - "Is classroom technology use at School Alpha consistent with constructivist principles and supportive of content standards?" OR
   - "Is the staff development program at School Beta adequately preparing teachers to use technology effectively?" OR
   - "Is technology used effectively in knowledge management and professional development at the Acme Workplace?")

3. Description of the Setting
4. Description of the Data-Gathering Process
5. Observations
6. Discussion and Conclusions

Recommended Procedure:

1. Read through at least one of the case study examples to get ideas for how you would like to present your analysis.
2. Identify the subject of your study, the central question that will shape the study, and the format for its presentation in newsgroups by March 3.
3. Conduct the study and write it up. Present it in web page format. List the url for the completed project as individuals, but on the final project in small groups—depending on what you and Paul Sparks decide. Some groups will want to collaborate on creating proposals to address the case study recommendations.
4. This project is due April 14. I will give you feedback on your project by email.

Figure 2.2. *EDC665 Case Study Analysis*

EDC665 Case Study Rubric

The following measurement criteria for each rubric are listed from unsatisfactory (D grade level) to outstanding (A grade level).

I Rubric for assessing the introductory material

- There is no introduction.
- The purpose is not identified.
- The introduction is present.
- Identification of the purpose and central questions is sketchy.
- The introduction provides an adequate context for the project.
- The purpose is identified through reference to one or more central questions.
- The introduction provides a well-developed context for the project.
- The significance of central questions is illustrated by references to course materials.

II Rubric for assessing descriptions of the setting and data collection process

- The narrative contains an incomplete or vague description of the setting, and no description of the data collection process.
- The narrative contains an adequate description of the setting, but an incomplete description of the data collection process.
- The narrative contains adequate descriptions of the case study setting and the data collection process.
- The narrative contains well-developed descriptions of the setting and the data collection process (which is built upon concepts from current research, theory, and course materials).

III Rubric for assessing the record of observations

- The narrative contains observations from only one perspective, or of a single type of data.
- The narrative contains observations from at least two sources.
- The narrative contains observations from multiple sources or includes qualitative and quantitative data.
- The narrative contains observations from multiple sources, includes qualitative and quantitative data, and makes references to models of appropriate practice which are supported by current research and theory.

IV Rubric for assessing the discussion, logic, and conclusions

- The discussion is incomplete or illogical, and conclusions are missing or unrelated to the central questions.
- The discussion is adequate, but conclusions—if present—do not match the central questions.
- The discussion seems complete.
- Conclusions are logical and address the central questions.
- The discussion seems complete. Conclusions are logical; the address the central questions, suggest possible strategies for addressing weaknesses, and are tied to the course work.

Figure 2.3. EDC665 Case Study Rubric

(continued)

V Rubric for assessing the presentation's clarity and style

At least three (3) of the following are true:

- The project contains multiple errors in grammar, spelling, or mechanics.
- The page layout is cluttered.
- Navigation between sections is unclear.
- APA format is not used in-text citations and bibliographical references to external resources

Two (2) of the following are true:

- The project contains multiple errors in grammar, spelling, or mechanics.
- The page layout is cluttered.
- Navigation between sections is unclear.
- APA format is not used in-text citations and bibliographical references to external resources

One (1) of the following is true:

- The project contains multiple errors in grammar, spelling, or mechanics.
- The page layout is cluttered.
- Navigation between sections is unclear.
- APA format is not used in-text citations and bibliographical references to external resources

All of the following are true:

1. The project contains no serious errors in grammar, spelling or mechanics.
2. The page layout facilitates understanding of the narrative.
3. Navigation between sections is clear.
4. APA format is used for in-text citations and bibliographical references to external resources.
5. To recieve an "A" on the project (>90%), the score must be 18 points or higher. This means that a "4" or "Exemplary" must be earned in at least 3 categories, with no lower than a "3" or "Accomplished" in the remaining two.

Figure 2.3.   (continued)

something that he or she suspected. The idea that this happens is especially timely in a context where the learner is consciously engaged in constructing a public entity (authentic demonstrations on the Web publicly—readily accessible), whether it is digital poetry, simulation design, virtual worlds, animation, music composition, reflective writing, building project(s), or Web sites.

Project-based Learning

Online courses lend themselves best to project-based learning because this gives students the opportunity to apply the content they have

Figure 2.4. EDC 665 Case Study Rubric
Rubric for Assessing Case Study—Part I of Final Project

	1 point	2 points	3 points	4 points
introductory material	There is no introduction. The purpose is not identified.	The introduction is present. Identification of the purpose and central questions is sketchy.	The introduction provides an adequate context for the project. The purpose is identified through reference to one or more central questions.	The introduction provides a well-developed context for the project. The significance of central questions is illustrated by references to course materials.
descriptions of the setting and data collection process	The narrative contains an incomplete or vague description of the setting, and no description of the data collection process.	The narrative contains an adequate description of the setting, but an incomplete description of the data collection process.	The narrative contains adequate descriptions of the case study setting and the data collection process.	The narrative contains well-developed descriptions of the setting and the data collection process (which is built upon concepts from current research, theory, and course materials).
record of observations	The narrative contains observations from only one perspective, or of a single type of data.	The narrative contains observations from at least two sources.	The narrative contains observations from multiple sources or includes qualitative and quantitative data.	The narrative contains observations from multiple sources, includes qualitative and quantitative data, and makes references to models of appropriate practice that are supported by current research and theory.

(continued)

Figure 2.4. *(continued)*

	1 point	2 points	3 points	4 points
discussion, logic, and conclusions	The discussion is incomplete or illogical, and conclusions are missing or unrelated to the central questions.	The discussion is adequate, but conclusions—if present—do not match the central questions.	The discussion seems complete. Conclusions are logical and address the central questions.	The discussion seems complete. Conclusions are logical; they address the central questions, suggest possible strategies for addressing weaknesses, and are tied to the course work.
presentation's clarity and style	At least three (3) of the following are true: • The project contains multiple errors in grammar, spelling or mechanics. • The page layout is cluttered. • Navigation between sections is unclear. • APA format is not used for in-text citations and bibliographical references to external resources.	Two (2) of the following are true: • The project contains multiple errors in grammar, spelling or mechanics. • The page layout is cluttered. • Navigation between sections is unclear. • APA format is not used for in-text citations and bibliographical references to external resources.	One (1) of the following is true: • The project contains multiple errors in grammar, spelling or mechanics. • The page layout is cluttered. • Navigation between sections is unclear. • APA format is not used for in-text citations and bibliographical references to external resources.	All of the following are true: • The project contains no serious errors in grammar, spelling or mechanics. • The page layout facilitates understanding of the narrative. • Navigation between sections is clear. • APA format is used for in-text citations and bibliographical references to external resources.

To receive an "A" on the project (>90%), the score must be 18 points or higher. This means that a "4" or "Exemplary" must be earned in at least 3 categories, with no lower than a "3" or "Accomplished" in the remaining two.

Philosophy	EDC 664 - Small Group Project 1	
Courses		Digital Portfolio
Faculty Profile	I want you folks to use the technology to think about	Small Group Projects 1&2
Contact Info	learning with the net. I am posting a subjective question	Assignment Calendar
Upcoming Events	outside your knowledge base and comfort zone and asking	
Grad School	you to learn something about it, share that knowledge with	Materials Texts
	others and try to reach consensus.	Example/Rubric
Resources		Objectives
Support	Your thinking about information you get from the web can	
Discussions	lead to extremely rich discussions. The web has all sorts of	Designing
Feature Videos	info from 'official sources,' fans, court documents and audio	Your Experience
Feature Projects	interviews among others. The range of modalities and	
	sources leads to thinking about the differences between	Learning
Services	learning now and 20 years ago.	Experiences
Feedback		
Honors	While I don't wish to tell you too much about the	Grading
Personal Life	educational objectives for this task (they are in my head,	
Site Map	but will wreck it for you if I say too much), I will say that	Printable Syllabus
	the activity has something to do with learning in the digital	
	age. It requires individual effort, group planning and a	
	synchronous discussion hopefully leading to some sort of	
	consensus.	

1. Learn something that will help YOU answer that question
2. Keep track of how you arrive at an answer/opinion/understanding and the resources you use.
3. Schedule a time to meet in Tapped-In with at least 4 classmates (4-5 groups should probably be formed, but part of this process involves YOU organizing yourself to get the work done.)
4. Try to arrive at a consensus within your group arguing your group's collective response to the question posed.

Figure 2.5.   Small Group Project

been learning to a real-world application. These projects give students the ability to make positive changes in their workplace or daily lives. Using project-based learning, teachers can better assess students' understanding rather than using traditional testing methods that are better suited to memorization or answering questions that rely on the regurgitation of text and reading without application. Project-based learning also encourages students to choose projects they are interested in and have a personal investment in, which, in turn, provides a higher quality of work.

Other topics rely more on Web searching and less on soul searching, but all projects are structured to develop problem-solving skills and a knowledge base of the subject matter. Project-based learning assignments show understanding of the "big idea." They create an opportunity for learners to take thoughts and apply them to their own lives and through the project show understanding of the big idea or application of course concepts. Learners have the opportunity to actively define issues and collaboratively build possible solutions.

People typically, no matter their learning style, benefit from actively participating in a project. Their learning is full of not only knowledge about the subject but of the application of the subject and how it works. Project-based learning is a good use of time as one learns to inquire, gather information, and reflect on the information. It allows the learner to learn about a skill while at the same time providing an opportunity to practice it.

These projects can be either individual or group based, simulating the everyday work in which students find themselves. These projects require students to visualize or simulate concepts and reveal in the learners' perceptions and misperceptions, understandings and misunderstandings. Visuals in a project can be done with digital media that students have access to in their workplace or at home. Using these visuals, such as digital photos or video, allows the teacher to see more of the students' thinking and understanding about the concepts behind the project.

Collaborative Project-based Learning Activities

Like the workplace, getting others involved in reviewing your ideas is important. We create an activity-driven experience for students to generate their own understanding based on the actions with the content and connections with their prior knowledge. Feedback from peers on these activities and projects is an essential part of their development. This delivery approach allows for integration of real-time information, multimedia, and ideas. Students can review the activity of others and offer ongoing feedback throughout the project. This "co-construction" of knowledge allows for shared learning in project work. These activities need to be rigorous enough to be meaningful but not overwhelming and not busywork. These virtual discussions make communication easier and allow for reflection and revision in the learning process. Students learn course work and technology skills in a way that also fosters valuable workplace competencies such as teamwork, communication, planning, and problem solving. Student participation in these discussions makes it possible for them to make use of new skills and information they did not have prior to taking the course.

Open-ended Assignments

Open-ended assignments allow for a look into how one thinks about the topic at hand. They clearly reflect the learning of the students and their ability to process information into concepts rather than in chunks, and they allow for the learner to move beyond concerns for finding the right or wrong answer while exploring the idea. To set the groundwork for a "mindful" learning experience (Langer, 1997), open-ended assignments should drive students' thoughts to the next step of information. Ideas and concepts are like a connect-the-dots exercise; as one idea makes sense, the learner is led to the next idea, and so on until the big idea is clear.

The original goals Pepperdine had when they launched open-ended Web assignments was to provide a platform where people were able to deal with issues of perspective, authorship, reliability, and validity, thereby increasing the authentic nature of the learning. Many educators have a growing concern about Internet use by students. We wanted to create a place where these concerns could be expressed and turned into a positive teaching and/or learning experience. You often hear, "but you need to know that the person who wrote the pages wasn't a kook and is an expert." Expertise and authorship issues are based on merit, not stature in the online world.

Therefore, using the far and local questions, In the gunfight at the OK Corral, who were the "bad" guys? Is Ned Kelly a hero? Were the Chicago Seven martyrs? allow for some Internet research, cognitive dissonance, and a discussion of point of view. The Chicago Seven question is less outside the experience and/or knowledge of our students, but from their culture, some students had very strong Vietnam-era feelings that clouded *their* perspective—very valuable in the discussion. That students are able to do both Web searching and soul searching and reflection is an essential component in the process of learning. For example, an interesting community activity is to assign the Ned Kelly question to a small group, report back assignment, and do the Chicago Seven in chat/synchronous session as a larger group moderated by the instructor. Instructors need to ask provocative questions and elicit evidence while facilitating the conversation.

Assignments should pose fully framed themes or questions, albeit purposefully vague. Like Haavind (2001), we found this increases the potential of eliciting a participant's real thinking on a topic. An example of an assignment from an introductory course is below:

Example:
This requires individual effort, group planning, and synchronous discussion, hopefully leading to some sort of consensus. While I don't wish to tell you too much about the educational objectives for this task (they are in my head but will wreck it for you if I say too much), I will say that the activity has something to do with learning in the Digital Age. Feel free to use the Net and traditional sources.

1. Think about the question (distributed in class).
2. Learn some things that will help *you* answer the question.
3. Keep track of how you arrive at an answer, opinion, or understanding and the resources you use.
4. Schedule time to meet in a synchronous environment with at least four classmates (three groups should probably be formed, but part of this process involves *you* organizing yourself to get the work done).
5. Try to arrive at a consensus within your group, arguing your group's collective responses to the question posed.
6. Develop a paragraph or two arguing your group's decision.
7. Email that paragraph to me, along with the names of your team when you are finished.
8. Wait until Monday; you will be notified to post your transcript and persuasive paragraph (I want to avoid polluting the work of another group).

As a few postings are made to the discussion, the instructor culls from the topic a theme worthy of careful focus or deeper digging and holds it up for the group to consider. Such an intervention might include three or four short quotes or paraphrases from earlier comments followed by a bit of explanation or clarification and then a single question to elicit more focused dialogue (Haavind, 2001). This allows for multiple perspectives and deeper reflection on the issues discussed. We believe you have to be responsive to the group and should not lecture online; instead, elicit meaningful discussions with questions based on

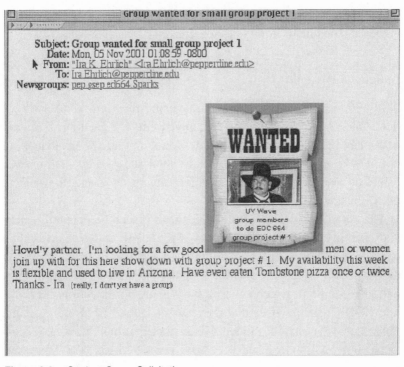

Figure 2.6.   *Student Group Solicitation*

students' observations and concerns. Allow students to determine the flow of the conversation where appropriate. Students should have opportunities to facilitate discussions as part of their assessment.

From this collective dialogue emerges a shared agenda that allows for more connections between the course content and their own workplace practices. This challenges students to use the Web tools in a number of ways. Students place the themes and highlights they glean from the course readings in newsgroups and a whiteboard in the synchronous environment, design Web sites, notes, virtual tours, and objects to create an order for discussion. This allows participants to think about their potential contributions of Web resources that can be posted or projected in these discussion environments to inform the discussion, support their contributions, and supplement, extend, and enrich course topics. Students can send images and/or pictures if they are embedded on Web pages by pushing URLs into the synchronous environment. Students also get practice in leadership and facilitating large and small groups online. For example, they may have to "herd" groups of students together and handle or minimize side conversations and distractions.

Building a Portfolio

In addition to synchronous and asynchronous online discussions, our students are also given the responsibility of creating, building, and maintaining their own Web site. Since one of the challenges of online learning is how to verify individual success, evaluating each student's Web portfolio is an efficient means of measuring student performance.

The emphasis on a student's Web site is placed on content, clarity, and usability rather than flashiness. As students move through their courses, they document their progress in a narrative form, accompanied with audio, graphics, animation, and video. A good deal of journaling is required, which encourages students to reflect on the skills, knowledge, and practices that they have acquired from the program. Portfolios often include students' best contributions in online discussions, best assignments, projects and contributions to collaborative team projects, and reflections on student work and the project processes.

There are many advantages to students publishing their own Web pages. Students must learn to create the Web page and upload it to a server, an additional learning experience, and for online learning, this is a common practice. Often, institutions provide learners with the tools for building their online portfolio. Other tools are available as well (even free ones), allowing students the same opportunity. New and exciting tools are searched out and updated by instructors and students. An instructor can have a list of resources on his or her Web site.

The requirement is for students to post the location of their assignment after it has been completed. In group projects, this type of work is excellent, as it provides members with an ability to instantaneously change information and post it, making it available for other team members to view and discuss. Students create and maintain their own Web site that peers are required to visit, as well as other members of the public. This public delivery enables all members of the class to review a student's work and give constructive feedback.

Online Lectures

Online learning lectures need to be structured in such a way that they are tied to the units or modules in your online course. Lectures can include video, music, skits, role-plays, quotes, case studies, and other assets, but certainly they do not have to fall into the traditional concept of lecturing. Moving to a more multimedia conceptualization, a lecture can be recorded and presented with a slide show or captured on digital video, reaching the auditory and visual learners. Many software programs can synchronize voice, music, and video with text presentation. Visuals complement voice and text, helping to get your message across. In presentations such as slide shows, use lots of charts, diagrams, and images to convey meaning. When you include links to additional resources and Web sites, you are teaching through presentation that there is much more knowledge to be sought after. Students can use this additional information to learn above and beyond the information you provide, helping to connect the bigger ideas in the course. Students should be encouraged to seek further sources of information to help provide clarification, extend concepts, and make meaning.

Metaphorical Language

Language and communications in online learning are very dynamic and have the potential of being extremely intense. Systems of symbolism, such as metaphors, stories, quotations, and reflections use emotions to create culture and non-verbal gestures for online language. There are unprecedented opportunities for personal creativity in expanding the range and variety of language online. The use of metaphorical language is one of the most powerful forms of communication and helps to build the sense of community within the online learning environment. Metaphors allow us to make connections by applying some degree of commonality to a subject perhaps otherwise obscure. They help to create a mental picture—a visual that not only gives clarity to meaning but also promotes retention of the new understanding being reached. Metaphorical language is also powerful in the sense that by naming an actual object and applying it to an idea, the object itself temporarily becomes part of the defining properties, yet retains its original meanings, which allows the connection in the mind to take place. For example, in figure 2.6 are actual online comments using metaphorical language in real-time (synchronous) discussion.

Field trips are also one strategic approach we utilize. Students are encouraged to visualize having class in a new and exciting environment: at the top of Mount McKinley, in a tree house, conversation pits, or at a cabin in the woods. The idea is to motivate them by placing them in an appealing setting. We've found it is best to explore and use environments or settings that have both meaning and motivation in relation to the content focus. Appropriate places describe things, locations, and phenomena that lack the traditional physical substance. Although they have no real substance or life equivalent, the persuasiveness of its representation allows students to respond as if it was based in reality.

Expression without Words

Instructors also must create metaphors, especially for non-verbal cues—for example, raising an eyebrow, leaning in, raising a hand, listening eagerly, smiling, and ROFLOL ("rolling on the floor, laughing out loud"). The instructor needs to build in the emotions and non-verbal cues in text-based synchronous environments to strengthen communication and mutual respect with his or her students.

Emoticons, Starlines, and Abbreviations

In spite of your best efforts to produce clear, inspiring messages, there will be times when you cannot communicate effectively using only words. When this happens, you might want to try some emoticons, little sideways ASCII renditions of human expressions that help to strengthen the tone of a given message. Here are a few examples— many of you will probably know, others you'd like to use:

- :-) User is happy; conveys positive meaning where the intent is unclear or where slight offense might be taken.

- ;-) User is winking; intended to tell recipient that the sender is joking or teasing. Note that this is not implying that you should tease your protégé, although some relationships may thrive on teasing or banter—be careful here.
- :-(User is unhappy; helps to put across disappointment, regret, or sympathy.
- :-/ User is embarrassed by his or her own mistake (think "urk!"). User may also be unsure or nervous.
- %-) User is confused but willing to take the time to understand.
- B-) User is proud (of self or recipient—the "B" is supposed to represent sunglasses).
- BTW. By the way.
- BRB. Be right back.
- BBIAB. Be back in a bit.
- IMHO. In my humble opinion.
- IMNSHO. In my not so humble opinion.
- LOL. Laughing out loud.
- TTYL. Talk to you later.
- AFK. Away from keyboard.

And, for presentation, these can be mixed with a few more humorous ones:

- WYSIWYG. What you see is what you get.
- WYSINWYG. What you see is not what you get.
- WYSINEUTWYG. What you see is not entirely unrelated to what you get.
- TNSTAAFL. There's no such thing as a free lunch.

Just about any common platitude is more humorous when abbreviated and then "played back" (Wear, 2000). Furthermore, using these guidelines for students can be helpful for avoiding frustration. Remember, the establishing of guidelines prior to the instructional and collaborative periods helps to solidify the community more fully, since each member knows the general format and expected process for communication.

Set Guidelines and Roles to Direct Communication

We found many students feel uncomfortable or frustrated when participating in discussions with no protocol. The purpose of these discussions is to provide students with a structured place each week to share emerging thoughts and questions on learning and, particularly, their role as a technology leader in their workplace. It is also a place to interact with other members of the learning community and the instructor around questions and issues that are raised in readings and course assignments, particularly about the links that students see between our readings and their own teaching context. Each participant in class is expected to incorporate information and insights gained from assigned readings and personal experiences into discussions. Guidelines are necessary in initial courses in the program. Students desire real clarity of how to contribute: when, what kind, but mostly, how much. If guidelines are not stated at the beginning of the course, students are not sure what might be expected.

Once a community is formed, it grows through continual interaction. Personal reflections are, of course, the most meaningful. However, instructors have found valid and effective ways to generate discussion within a group by setting up roles. In our designed discussion processes, which allow everyone a voice and encourage listening and understanding, our students feel safe and can explore issues openly, knowing that their status in the group is that of an equal who can have valid input. Successful cooperative groups depend on each member taking an active role, which assures the group functions efficiently and effectively, with each member "pulling his or her own weight." There are a variety of ways to ensure this. One is assigning specific roles to each member. General roles we have used include summarizer, facilitator, technician or researcher, insighter, and critic, to name a few. For example, the summarizer in each group should highlight two or three main ideas or significant insights from his or her group's discussion. However, in using these roles it is vital to allow students the choice of the roles among themselves, as well as to keep the role titles at a minimum. Using roles for discussion generation will only be effective if the student is able to connect his or her own reflections and observations to the role.

These roles allow students to examine a discussion from a particular perspective. Students should be involved in selecting their own roles, and should have a sense of zeal within the role, in order to discuss their topic prospectively and reflectively. Students know ahead of the discussion what their roles are. This gives participants time to contemplate their role and make notes for comments in later discussion. It might also benefit the group members if the roles are rotated throughout the group to allow each student the experience of leading the discussion through, being the herder, keeping folks on track, and summarizing the discussion in order to appreciate the need for full participation so that the group can be effective in their interactions. Table 2.1 provides a clear illustration of the community roles.

Table 2.1. Key Community Roles

Type of Leadership	Definition	Typical Activities
Coordination	Keepers of the community	Organize events, talks to members, keeps the pulse of the community
Networking	Keepers of relationships	Connect people, weave the community's social fabric
Facilitation	Keepers of conversations	Set agendas, watch over conversations, keep notes, provide pointers and summaries
Documentation	Keepers of the repository	Organize information in order to document practices, update and clean up the knowledge base
Expertise	Keepers of the heritage	Thought leaders and recognized experts uphold and dispense the accumulated wisdom of the community
Learning	Keepers of insights	Watch for nuggets, collect emerging pieces of knowledge, standards, and lessons learned
Inquiry	Keepers of questions	Notice emergent questions, keep them alive, outline a learning agenda, and shepherd "out-of-the-box" initiatives
Boundary	Keepers of connections	Connect the community to other communities or constituencies, act as brokers and translators
Institution	Keepers of organizational constituencies	Maintain links with other organizational constituencies, in particular the official hierarchy

Source: Smith, 2001.

Synchronous Discussion

Real-time discussion is important if you want your online course to be dynamic and more than an online correspondence course. Real-time discussions are becoming one of the most popular teaching methods for encouraging online interactions between students. Table 2.2 demonstrates the various forms of synchronous discussion resources. The goal of the discussion is usually to promote thinking about the content and its applications. Since most factual questions are forgotten by the learner (Shiever, 1991), research shows that high-level questions will elicit higher-level processes (Batson, 1981; McKenzie, 1972; Taba, 1966), and also 80 to 85 percent of what students learn by questioning is retained. In the online environment, we have found that centering questions and expanding questions will produce the most depth in online discussion.

Text-based discussion has its own specific dialect and colloquialism; as students become more comfortable in the text-based conversation setting, they become increasingly able to develop questions, phrases, and reword text before hitting enter to express their thoughts, emotions, frustrations, and even gestures using symbolic or representative techniques. Written, text-based formats provide the opportunity for deliberate reflection and editing rather than impulsive outbursts. This environment

Table 2.2. Synchronous Discussion Resources

Synchronous Tool	Application	Examples
Chat	Group social interaction Touching base Covering main ideas	Yahoo Chat, mIRC, Trillian
Instant Messenger (IM)	One on one chat Checking ideas	AIM, Yahoo, MSN, ICQ
MUD and MOO	Social Interaction	Tapped In MediaMoo TecfaMOO
Video conferencing, Audio conferencing	Important Meetings	NetMeeting
Whiteboard	Brainstorming	Centra, Blackboard, WebCT, TopClass
Application sharing	Group writing projects Simulations Demonstrations Software training	Webex

has with it no "rulebook" of behavioral text language. Language as text-based input also has with it its own drawbacks, but with eager students, they are quickly overcome. One of these problems may be the typing ability and speed of students. Since people generally speak faster than they type, students may find the synchronous discussion setting to be initially frustrating. Yet, we find that students increase in their speed as well as their ability to articulate (via text) the more they participate in this learning environment. There are other areas of frustration as well that can be quickly and easily avoided with introductory instructions in the synchronous process. Below are some simple guidelines to manage traffic in the conversation that can be given to students to deter the amount of frustration in synchronous discussion environments.

1. When "speaking," use a leader (e.g., ". . .") at the end of a statement when not finished with a thought. Anything in excess of three lines of text will be too much, so you must divide up your discussion comments into smaller segments so you do not lose the audience while they are waiting for you to type it in. Also, you run the risk that it will be lost as other comments come pouring in right after, comments that were waiting in the queue while yours was being typed and sent. This makes the discussion more fragmented.

2. As a "listener," do not interrupt. Wait until the speaking person has finished expressing his or her thought before replying. Be patient and work at being comfortable with momentary silences, as they are to be expected. Sometimes responses from two or more participants will happen at virtually the same time. Let's say this happens to Austin and Jake. Jake could step back for a moment and let Austin know it is okay to continue by saying something like "Austin, go ahead." After Austin finishes, he needs to return the conversation to Jake with a "Jake, what do you think?" or "Jake, do you have more to add?"

3. Stay on topic and share only messages that are relevant to the subject of the discussion group until everyone that wants to say something about that topic has spoken. Do not perpetuate off-topic comments. If someone makes an inappropriate comment, do not add more noise by replying to it in the discussion.

4. If you have specific ideas, resources, or questions you want to share during a discussion, type them into a word-processing document and then copy and paste them into the discussion. Most people can copy and paste faster than they can type.

5. Don't worry about spelling. We will assume that all of your misspellings and grammatical mistakes are typo errors, so don't try to go back and correct them.

6. Use common abbreviations acronyms and symbols to simplify your typing. If you are going to use an abbreviation often that may not have a common understanding, define it the first time you use it.

7. Remember that it is easy to misinterpret words when you have no accompanying facial, body, or tone expressions to give additional meaning to those words. Try not to assign a tone to the person speaking. You can use smiley faces :-) to indicate that you're smiling and CAPS to make a strong point. If you do not understand what someone else is trying to say or think you may be misinterpreting what they have said, state your interpretation with a question, "Madeline, are you saying that—?" You can add adjectives and/or descriptors of emotions in the text, too.

8. Use page numbers when referring to books to help others find the place of a graphic, quote, or idea quickly.

9. Be civil. Please refrain from inappropriate comments and personal attacks. If you disagree with something someone has said, do not become emotional; instead, politely justify your position.

10. Remember that every person comes to this environment at different levels of ability and comfort. Be patient and encouraging to create a comfortable learning experience for everyone.

Figure 2.7 represents an example of an encouraging synchronous conversation.

Asynchronous Discussion

While real-time chat is a very valuable way for students to communicate in your online class, the most used method for communi-

Synchronous Interaction
Ana (A): I've been struggling on how to simplify data and format the presentation. Your work is guiding me and getting me to settle down.
Stephanie (S): That is weird for me to hear (but nice) because I honestly have looked to your work on so many past projects as my guide...and thank you again for that in case I ever forgot to tell you :)
(A): I really like your students' pros and cons. It shows there honest and non- bias concerns in their day to day environment.
(S): LOL, the pros and cons thing seemed like the only possible choice I had for presenting this info...and I was actually unsure about it, seems so plain and unsophisticated to me I guess...your viewpoint is helpful
(A): These were some of the concerns the children and I discussed in one of our meetings. Of course my environment does not have laptops... We like to brainstorm the 'what ifs?". Glad to hear that these are real issues.
(S): They are real and very serious...and parents are expressing many similar comments when I speak to them...come to think of it, I should have been writing their comments down all along, not just the students...
(A): Steph, curious about your opinion too, Who really pushed for the laptops - the parents or the teachers?
(S): Neither...the school administration spent some time from what I understand visiting a couple of other private schools up north who had similar programs that were deemed successful. The teachers, from what I can gather, were as a collective whole, not a part of the process, which I think was a grave mistake...
(A): Was the curriculum set up to integrate way before the purchase of the laptops or did they get the laptops before the integration? Some high-end schools like to get laptops because it creates a nice Public Relations with the Community... a 'hip' school per se. Do you think that this school had this in mind first
(S): I think you hit the nail on the head with the public relations thing...what has happened here in our little town of Tampa is that my old school (Tampa Preparatory) has been planning and building this spectacular state-of-the art nationally recognized brand new ~$30 million school (to be opened this fall) so Berkeley a couple of years ago freaked and had to come up with something that was "spectacular" to compete...well the laptop program I guess seemed the public relations agenda of choice (for the administration any ways). Was the curriculum set up to integrate these laptops? No, in fact they still use the old curriculum and are trying to mesh the laptops in to them which seems pretty difficult tome...
(A): The computer experts... Are they technical or educational or both? How are the teachers skills in technology? Do they follow the official or classical approach? Are they constructivists?
(S): Honestly, I am not sure which philosophy of education they follow since they don't actually teach...good thought though...
(A):It's just funny that they were asked to purchase the laptops with outthinking of the personal needs of the child, basic- storing and necessities. The physical environment would be important to consider before implementation.. don't you think?

Figure 2.7.   Student–Student Synchronous Discussion

cation will be in the form of asynchronous discussions. Examples of this kind of discussion would be email and newsgroups, and table 2.3 demonstrates the various forms of asynchronous discussion resources. These discussions take place outside of real time and require the instructor to set up a newsgroup or list service and have

Table 2.3. Asynchronous Discussion Resources

Asynchronous Tool	Learning Application	Examples
Email	Private conversations Submitting assignments containing sensitive info	Outlook, Outlook Express Eudora, Entourage
Newsgroups	For deep discussions Student questions Reaching consensus	Netscape, Outlook Express
Web Pages (HTML)	Web Portfolios Syllabus Publishing	Dreamweaver, Adobe GoLive, Frontpage
Listserv	Communication of changes Announcements Polling	Yahoo Groups

students become members or "subscribers" to the service. Figure 2.8 is an example of a threaded discussion, while figure 2.9 is a response within the discussion. An instructor can post messages to the board in the form of questions and ask for students to respond, initiating discussion about certain topics or readings to do with the content. At

Subject	To/From	Total	Date	Lengt
▽ Brain Drain (Interesting Article)	Cathy ...	43	10/22/00 12:13 PM	64
Re: Brain Drain (Interesting Arti...	Kris Te...		10/22/00 2:44 PM	98
Re: Brain Drain (Interesting A...	Jessic...		10/22/00 7:00 PM	126
Re: Brain Drain (Interesting...	Kris Te...		10/23/00 3:33 PM	35
Re: Brain Drain (Interesti...	Jennife...		10/23/00 5:12 PM	81
Re: Brain Drain (Interesting Arti...	kyle w...		10/22/00 5:03 PM	81
Re: Brain Drain (Interesting Arti...	Marty ...		10/22/00 6:48 PM	93
Re: Brain Drain (Interesting A...	Jennife...		10/22/00 7:48 PM	52
Re: Brain Drain (Interesting...	Tom S		10/23/00 7:43 PM	16
Re: Brain Drain (Interesting Arti...	Jessic...		10/22/00 6:54 PM	87
Re: Brain Drain (Interesting Arti...	Linda P...		10/23/00 9:08 PM	77
Re: Brain Drain (Interesting Arti...	Patrici...		10/23/00 9:33 PM	40
Re: Brain Drain (Interesting Arti...	Cathy ...		10/25/00 5:16 PM	93
Re: Brain Drain (Interesting A...	Jennife...		10/25/00 6:15 PM	138
Re: Brain Drain (Interesting A...	Jessic...		10/25/00 8:13 PM	105
Re: Brain Drain (Interesting...	Cathy ...		10/30/00 7:50 PM	113
Re: Brain Drain (Interesting A...	Kris Te...		11/12/00 1:21 PM	132
Re: Brain Drain (Interesting A...	kyle w...		10/28/00 3:30 PM	22
Re: Brain Drain (Interesting...	Kris Te...		11/12/00 1:26 PM	33
Re: Brain Drain (Interesti...	kyle w...		11/12/00 4:57 PM	39
Re: Brain Drain (Intere...	Jennife...		11/13/00 5:47 PM	61

Figure 2.8.   *Threaded Discussion*

Welcome to the Community Room, where you are always a legitimate member of the activity system in play.

Adittional discussion rooms can be found to the south and north (see below).

```
(S)outh  . . . . . . . . . .the GREEN room
(N)orth . . . . . . . . . . .the BLUE room
OUT  . . . . . . . . . . . .Pepperdine Third Floor Offices
(U)p . . . . . . . . . . . . .the TREEHOUSE
```

What is here? Whiteboard, Supplies, Clock. a mural, Ms. Coffee, pretzels, tangerines, black pot-bellied stove, plant, table, chairs, big bubbling hot tub, comfy couch, conversation pit, windows.

RobinL asks, "I understand trying to create a situation neutral theory, but isn't it at odds with the context-important points L&W make?"

LucyL says, "I work in an academy so we do work place learning."

SuzanneO says, "True"

You say, "I think before we can do that we might need to take a look at what makes "schooling" a special case."

SuzanneO exclaims, "Great idea!"

You say, "it isn't a situation neutral theory"

You say, "oh I get what you mean, never mind"

HankLS says, "They say that learning is socially based but leave out the primary social venue in this country for learning"

KevinBR agrees with Robin and is not sure the point is to do a "situation neutral theory" but a complexly concrete threorizing.

KevinBR says, ". . . to use just a few L&W jargon terms."

LeeAnn [guest] says, ". . . and that theorizing needs to be separated before it is applied to any given setting."

You [to Hank]: "some folks might not agree that the primary social venue is schooling. Kids learn a lot outside of school and adults do too. Most of you work in non-K-12 settings, no?"

Figure 2.9. Chat

the same time, students can also post messages to the newsgroup to initiate conversations about topics of interest and relevance to the readings, resources that they find, or even questions they have about a concept they do not understand.

Often it is beneficial for the group to establish some rules or "norms" for the threaded discussion area or newsgroup and the way that people will respond to one another. Things to keep in mind when creating these norms:

1. Quality posts are more helpful than quantity posts. Posts of "way to go" or "I agree" should be sent to the individual personally rather than posted in the threaded discussion area or newsgroup.

2. Students as well as the instructor should respond to the postings of peers. This relates to intellectual questions, misconceptions, and cries for help—not just emotional reactions. Stay on topic and share only messages that are relevant to the subject of the discussions of the group. Do not perpetuate off-topic comments. If someone makes an inappropriate comment, do not add more noise by replying to it in the discussion. Instead, model appropriate, inoffensive ways to correct people.

3. Students should be encouraged to remember that when they are posting, they should be trying to move the conversation forward in a positive manner.

4. Students should remember to sign their name to what they write and remember to spell and grammar check what they write before they send it to the group. Don't say anything online you wouldn't want to say in public.

5. Always use a clear subject. Erase the default one that is created for you (re: whatever the last subject was) and type a new one that really does say something about your message. If everyone does this, you can quickly skim the titles of the messages and then jump in where you find something interesting. This enables you and other students to locate discussion topics and follow the threads of the discussion easier for later reference.

6. Use common abbreviations, acronyms, and symbols to simplify your typing. If you are going to use an abbreviation often that may not have a common understanding, define it the first time you use it.

Your students may want to set up an email discussion group listing with a service such as Yahoo in order to communicate among themselves. If using a service like this, one of your students can set up a group in which the other students can become members. It is important, however, to make certain that no members of the group are inadvertently left off of the email listserv group. This could cause very hurt feelings down the road and cause damage to the "community of practice." This allows students to communicate issues here rather than in the class discussion areas. Students frequently use multiple communication tools at the same time. It is not uncommon for small groups of students to be discussing an issue via Instant Messenger in the background while a professor leads a discussion in the synchronous chat tool. Here they can swap files, send jokes, and talk about non-school stuff, which helps build community within your group. They might decide to allow you as the instructor membership as well in order for you to be able to communicate with the group, but remember, it has to be their decision to let you into the "club." In the past this has been a helpful layer of insight for me as an instructor. I seldom post as I want it to be their space. However, it does allow me to post to clarify misunderstandings early before more misinformation and frustration build around an issue.

Benefits of Virtual Discussions

Virtual discussions have five main benefits:

- Promotes community.
- Develops resourcefulness.
- Generates interaction.
- Provides immediate feedback.
- Allows collaborative activity.

Reading other people's posts is like listening to a conversation about a topic, which offers some advantages that listening to a lecture does not. The back and forth and the exposure to similar ideas in different guises help one learn. Posting to a discussion forces us to put our thoughts into words. This imposes a discipline on what may have started as vague notions. Some ideas evaporate under the effort of writing them out. Others evolve and become stronger. In order to learn a subject well, one must learn to communicate about it. Discussions are one place to practice that skill and to see others practicing it as well in purposeful discussions. That is precisely what is needed, in our view.

There is a necessity, in writing, for the sort of spontaneous exploration that some online formats promote. I think online contributions, if appropriately guided, can be a positive influence on the development of other essential writing skills. The sustained, focused thought required for a paragraph must be demanded and practiced in some circumstances — and it seems to me that an online course really ought to include an environment for the sort of contributions that promote this kind of skill. Unlike formal papers, discussions focus on communicating with peers rather than with the instructor, so they broaden one's experience of communication. A student who participates in a discussion is playing an active part in his or her own education, coming into contact with a variety of views, and experiencing the kind of fitful and uncertain progress that really characterizes the work of the mind but is often concealed by linear, well-organized lectures. We don't just like students to "talk" just for talking's sake. So, focused discussion questions, like the sample assignment shown in figure 2.10, are an excellent way to keep the conversation focused on the course material.

- Choose a partner.

- Pick a topic from the box provided on your syllabus page under this assignment.

- Read the course readings associated with your topic (chapter or pages that were provided to help you understand the topic).

- Write summary of the topic you read. Develop one or two thought provoking questions based on the material. Place these at the end of your summary.

- Post the summary and question in the threaded discussion area as a new thread.

- Check the thread periodically, (at least twice a week) to see if people have responded. Keep the discussion going by replying to those students that respond to you a.k.a. monitoring threaded discussion.

- On your own, review the other threads posted by your classmates. Then, review the course readings and content about those topics.

- Select and reply to at least two classmates questions that you find interesting and reply to those questions. Integrate course readings and content into your

Figure 2.10. Sample Threaded Discussion Assignment

Every time a student posts, they need to respond also to at least two of their peers, and this needs to be expressed as a norm for the program. Instructors should be in approximately 20 percent of posts, based on research on the most effective online courses. Students look for the presence of the instructor. But the instructor needs to be responsive to the groups' needs, to support creativity and inventiveness, and to encourage the collective direction students take with content in the course. Discussions should not be dictated by the instructor but should be a safe place for students to explore course material, its application, and the reflective process. Instructors can do a great deal to provide a safe and secure environment for student interaction by handling inappropriate behavior with good judgment. I have found that as an instructor, I need to inject the same humor and ease online that I use face to face, but I see the challenge is in getting the balance right.

CONCLUSIONS

In analyzing the effectiveness of online discussion groups in learning environments, it is vital to keep each portion of the learning environment intact. All the pieces mentioned in this discussion are crucial for establishing meaningful learning in the online environment. Real-time discussion in learning cannot stand alone to bring about the most meaningful learning experience. Each piece fits together to formulate a learning environment that encourages internalization of knowledge to effect a change within the learner. The discussions are only one piece of the puzzle and provide one element of several that support the depth of the learning that takes place within the program.

These discussions have enhanced our insights around the sociopsychological implications of Web-based learning environments. Pepperdine's virtual discussions have proven successful, thus far, in achieving the learning community that is central to its philosophy. The program has facilitated collaboration and built repertoire through joint enterprise (e.g., collaboration and mutual accountability), mutual engagement (e.g., working together, relationship building, and maintenance), and shared repertoire (e.g., personal stories, artifacts, and experiences). Figure 2.11 is adapted from Etienne Wenger's book *Communities of Practice* (1998) and illustrates the three multi-faceted

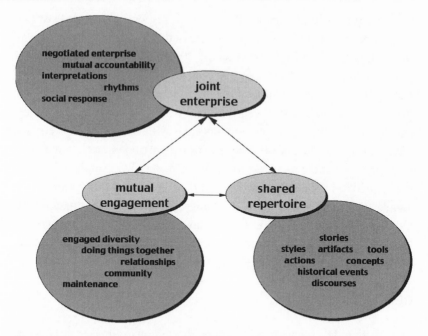

Figure 2.11. Characteristics of a Community of Practice (Wenger, 1998)

dimensions that distinguish a community from a community of practice. The program continues to open a wider range of expression for students, helps them "find" their own voice, simplifies assignment and assessment logistics, and increases the convenience, flexibility, and overall enjoyment of the learning process. These are the broad terms of the impact of emerging technology for virtual discussion on the students as well as other possible factors that have brought higher academic performance.

Because online learning environments and synchronous discussions have the potential for being the most innovative learning tool in technology to date, careful consideration of its implementation and application must be used in order to gain its full potential. In our experience, a more adequate account of knowledge and learning is to be found in a social, contextual environment that recognizes the creative and spontaneous nature of the human mind.

CHAPTER 3

Foundation for Instructional Screen Design

The design must blend what is engaging with what is effective. Just because a lesson is engaging does not mean it is effective in causing understanding.

—Grant Wiggins and Jay McTighe, *Understanding by Design*

With the increased use of computers to present instructional information to both groups and individuals, it is important to consider how we can best aid the learning that is desired. Screens of information are presented in tutorial software and for group instruction using presentation software. With the growth in the use of presenting information "screen by screen," we need to examine how the information is presented in order to better serve the learner. The screens rely heavily on the "visual perception" of the learner. Since this is the case, we suggest that more than aesthetic and visual design principles need to be considered when designing screens of instructional material. Elements of Gestalt theory could also be used to inform the design.

Why refer back to Gestalt theory? The laws of perception developed by Gestaltists can aid the coherent creation of screen design, which should help learners interpret and remember the materials presented. Kohler (1947) and Koffka (1935) stated that visual fields are organized into visual patterns, which are grouped according to the laws of perception. Moore and Fitz (1993) suggested the use of Gestalt theory to inform the instructional design of visual printed materials. We suggest that these principles cannot only inform how to design instruction on the printed page but also on the computer screen. Even though these laws can inform text and still graphics on the computer screen, computer technology includes the use of techniques, such as animation, that are not possible on the printed page. Gestalt theory can also be used to inform the use of these techniques.

The laws discussed in this section include figure-ground relationships, proximity, similarity, and simplicity. In addition, Gestalt theory states that what is perceived by the individual is understood by the individual as a whole, or *gestalt*, not as component parts. The computer screen, whether it is on a monitor or projected, is a visual field. As a visual field these principles can be applied with the intention of increasing the educational effectiveness. These laws can be applied to both text and graphics.

FIGURE-GROUND RELATIONSHIPS

The first law considered here is the figure-ground law. A figure must be distinct from the background. This is often a problem with the computer screen. The use of color on the computer screen can interfere with the distinction between the figure and the ground. For example, in several presentations we have observed, there is a background containing clouds with the text in blue, which often blended into the blue portions of the cloud background. This makes the text difficult to read. Complex backgrounds are often so busy that the text becomes lost to the learner. This should be considered when designing a screen. Text and objects, which are important for instruction, should be clearly defined from the background. The learner should not have to work to separate the instructional material (e.g., text or graphic) from the background. This interferes with the ease with which the learner should be able to interpret the material.

In addition, when we consider text, the font type and size affect their distinction from the background. This is particularly a problem with the computer because the light is emitted from the screen rather than reflected, as it is on paper. Letters on the screen are made up of small dots of light called pixels. These pixels emit light, which can cause blurring, particularly with small spidery letters composed of thin lines. The learner then has difficulty in decoding what the letters are, hindering his or her understanding of the material.

The concept of clarity between the figure and ground also affects how graphics should be used in the screen presentation. This relationship explains how individuals can perceive different things from the same illustration. For example, there is the drawing that is often used that can be interpreted as a vase or two faces. The interpretation depends partly on the individual's experience, partly on what is perceived as the background, and partly on what is perceived as the foreground. Therefore, graphics should be clearly designed to eliminate ambiguity about which is the foreground and which is the background. In other words, you should not be able to reverse the foreground and the background on an instructional graphic.

Proximity

The law of proximity states that items that are placed near one another appear to be a group. This can affect how one perceives a screen. This automatic grouping of objects placed together can cause confusion if objects are misplaced. For example, when more than one graphic is labeled on a screen, the label should be clearly placed with the appropriate graphic. If the placement of labels is unclear, the learner will have difficulty deciding which label belongs with which object. In order to avoid the ambiguity, it is important to pay close attention to how objects and labels are placed. Labels are not the only text affected by proximity.

A greater amount of space between letters or words can isolate sections of the text. Depending upon the intent this can either hinder or help the learner's understanding of the information on the screen. For example, in figure 3.1, two concepts are presented—the main content and then additional links to information—text for each is separated so that the difference between the two is clearly defined both verbally and visually. This helps the learner by providing not just verbal but visual cues. If key points in a presentation are grouped closely without visual cues, such as numbering or lettering (as sometimes occurs), the decoding by the learner is more difficult because there are no visual discrimination cues provided. Proximity can also inform other aspects of screen design.

Proximity can inform how the viewer classifies objects within the screen presentation. If we want learners to form a concept that includes

---

Cycle Document

Your document should include the following sections. Most sections will probably need between one and two pages each to give the information. It should include:

- **Goal**
  What were you hoping to accomplish in your own practice and in the surrounding environment? What problem did you see that needed to be fixed? From what research base did you design a possible solution?
- **Activities**
  What did you try? With whom did you try it? What happened?
- **Data**
  What data did you collect? When did you collect it? From whom did you collect it? Although it is not necessary to put every piece on your web site, include summaries and representative examples of your data.
- **Insights**
  What did you learn as you reflected on the data gathered during your activities? What connections can you make to your readings in other classes or in your outside reading? What did you learn about yourself, your practice, and the people involved in your ARP?
- **Surprises**
  Any surprises? Did you learn anything . . . see anything . . . realize anything . . . that you didn't expect? Any new twists to your ARP?
- **Where to go from here**
  As a result of your reflection, what do you see yourself trying in the next cycle? This should be based on both what happened in your first cycle and your research. You may end up doing some more reading based on your first cycle results. This section will become the rough draft for your goal section in the next cycle document.

Grading
When determining a grade, I will look at the richness of your experience in your ARP, your understanding of the ARP process, your fulfillment of the requirements stated above.

Figure 3.1. *Action Research Project (ARP) Cycle Document*

several types of objects, and those objects appear different on the surface, we can group them together as exemplars to aid the student in the formation of the concept. In this manner, by putting objects close together we help the student think about how the items in the grouping are alike.

Similarity

Another aspect of Gestalt theory which can help provide guidance for screen design is similarity. The law of similarity can be used to guide students to key phrases, words, or illustrations. According to Kohler (1947), information reconstruction can be aided by directing attention to specific items in a visual display. This becomes quite easy with computer presentations. Objects or text that is similar will be seen as a whole. This aspect of Gestalt theory explains why attention is drawn to underlined or highlighted words in printed text. On the computer screen, we can do more than underline or highlight. Words and phrases can be animated by different colors, and flash brighter and dimmer. These characteristics help to draw the learner's attention to key words or phrases because they are different from the surrounding text. When the text is all the same, learners will not have the advantage of the cues that are possible using various techniques.

Simplicity

When learners are presented with visuals, there is an unconscious effort to simplify what is perceived into what the viewer can understand. According to Kohler (1947) and Koffka (1935), individuals simplify what they perceive according to their previous experiences and their current expectations. If the visual presented is complex, the viewer will simplify what is perceived into terms he or she can understand. This indicates that designers of screen presentations should consider starting out with simple graphics that individuals could perceive and then interpret in very similar ways. The more complex the visual presented and the more extraneous information presented in the visual, the more likely an individual is to interpret the visual in a way that was unintended. In some instructional materials presented via computer complex drawings or photographs, present more visual information than is needed by the individual to learn the intended information from the visual. When considering the use of visuals, the designer should consider using graphics and photographs that limit visual distractions. For example, if students are learning about different types of architectural columns, it would be more effective to use drawings of the column types or photographs that show only the columns. Photographs of buildings, which contain other things (such as trees, gardens, people, and so forth) would be better used after initial instruction presented the types of columns without the distracting elements. While the law of simplicity states that individuals will simplify what they perceive, the designer should avoid the possibility that the individual can simplify the visual in a way other than the one desired for the instruction.

Some Thoughts for the Laws of Perception

Motivation organizes perception. Visitors to our Web pages are constructing their own visual fields depending on their need in the moment. This derives from Kohler's work in problem solving: His experimental subject, an ape, saw a stool, pole, and bananas and was motivated to reorganize the field to meet his need to eat. If I visit a site and don't find anything like I usually use in my teaching, I move on. Another person who teaches the same classes may visit the site looking for something new and different. Thus, I am motivated to seek confirmation and similarity, and the other person seeks stimulation and change.

Consequently, in pilot testing Web pages carefully designed with attention to the laws of perception, we must ask ourselves about the motivating needs that our visitors will be attempting to meet. These needs give rise to gathering data about users and revising Web pages to meet the most common needs. Compromise is generally part of the process; there is no one "right" way. The process of designing and revising is the end.

Content-Organization Strategies

Create discovery learning whereby learners click on something to find the right answer. Every two to three screens of reading should be followed by an interactive exercise to help put the content of the reading into a context for the reader.

- Substance of course needs to be easy to find and clear.
- Send out a video on CD-ROM rather than using the Web for video for those with slower connections.
- Label your site with "best viewed in" suggestions (e.g., "best viewed in Microsoft Explorer").

- Provide a phone number for tech support and contact names of people who will support your program. Provide a phone number of a real live person for online learners to ask technical questions.
- Chunk text and activities among text, including relevant and interesting content.
- Develop and provide a FAQ section or help section for the students to refer to at first, especially if you have new students each term.
- Have tutorials for writing a research paper and properly formatting it, having clear instructions on things as simple as:
  - how to use copy and paste functions
  - how to use the online library
  - how to post a comment in the threaded discussion
  - what they should do if they haven't received their book in the mail yet
  - what to do if their computer shuts down in the middle of an exam, etc. These can really go a long way toward alleviating the anxiety, so they can focus on the course content. Consider including these instructions in audio or video format.
- Give them an online place for them to submit problems. If you have continuing students, this might only be necessary in your introductory courses.

Organizing Online Presentations

You always have to start with the end in mind; try to identify three to four main points, not fifteen or twenty. Ask yourself, What do I want students to take away from my course—skills, contents, and knowledge understandings? Summarize your purpose for the course and use it throughout the process to focus your efforts, so they are relevant, effective, and aligned with your purpose. When you are comfortable then you can experiment and try what works for you based on your personality.

The principles outlined here are meant to guide, not constrain. They provide a starting structure. In your online presentations, use a basic outline that includes:

- Opener
- Transition

- Purpose statement
- Body of your text
- No more than three to four points
- Wrap up—end memorably

Introduction

- Set up the audience, use humor and visualization—an image to hook, stories, things of human interest, quotations, upbeat music— to set the mood. Combined with images, this sets an environment that is comfortable.

Open Effectively

- Have a hook, a point of relevance.
- Body of your text has to be clear. Compelling, interesting anecdotes and simple quotations can be used to elaborate.

Middle

- Central message and ideas for outcome.

End

- Refers back to main themes and ideas, then interaction.

Linking and Summing Up

- Give clear signals when you are changing ideas.
- Logical flow.
- Visual and auditory transitions between old ideas and new ideas. How do they link things together?
- Summarize each major point before the next point and begin to weave them together.
- Use repetition to recap and reinforce the major points.
- Restate at end of each section with different words to sound fresh.
- Give signals that the end is near: "for my final point…".

Points of Organizational Importance

- Visualize how you want the audience to respond.
- Order is critical.
- Choose an appropriate structure.
- Style needs to follow natural speech patterns.
- Match speaking style with your visual medium.
- Several different ways to introduce a main point.
- Chronological or "order of importance" are options.
- Start with a point that gives the strongest impression.
- In a sense, you're creating a "spiraling hierarchy," where key points are interwoven and summarized to show how they connect with one another. This allows students to approach the material from different angles or slightly different perspectives.
- Give your narrative a storytelling format when writing.
- Beginning, middle, and end.

PRINCIPLES OF GRAPHIC DESIGN FOR YOUR "WEB OFFICE" OR CLASS

General layout principles are critical in creating effective and powerfully clear communication. Create a memorable, informative experience. If your design is poor, it may lead your audience to miss messages or become frustrated. Design must be consistent. Viewers unconsciously detect inconsistencies, and this leads to major confusion. Once you confuse them, you lose them.

Be consistent with text and graphics and treat similar items in a simple manner. The effect becomes jarring and distracting if no theme or consistency is present. You do not want to create a ransom-note effect with fifteen different fonts and special effects that are not aligned with the message, because then the focus is more on the form of the message than the content of the message. There is no substitute for substance.

Graphics need some connection and consistency to the message. There is a basic difference between consistency and uniformity. Consistency says there are certain elements in the same place. You may want to try using style sheets that will help establish a consistency in colors and size of font, for example. This way, both horizontally and vertically each page in your course has the same look and feel.

When considering your graphics, ask yourself, Does it contribute to a powerful transmission of the intended message? Does it work? If so, then let it break a few of these rules. Keep the focus and consistency of your theme and message. Be wary of clip art—the eye attacks clip art differently than it does graphic images. Only use clip art if it really fits or if you are absolutely desperate.

For your convenience there are many photo CDs. They not only give you images but flexibility in choosing color of background, so they absolutely blend in. You can find image CDs where most software is sold but make sure they are photographs, not clip art. Also, an inexhaustible supply of items can be found at Google.com. Simply type in the subject and select the tab titled Images on the top, then check for copyright and determine if it is royalty free. If copyrighted, write the holder of the copyright and request permission to use the image. Another avenue is to search for sites specializing in royalty-free images. When choosing images, bear in mind that you will need images of a high quality, not "bit" images that become pixilated when you stretch them. If you find an image on Google or a similar source and it's in the range of 7k, it is likely to smear when stretched.

One caution—do not put images up on the edge of the page unless, for instance, it is a person walking onto the page to imply motion; images need some white space around them. Implied motion is a very big and powerful idea in graphic presentation. The mind follows the apparent or implied direction of eyes in the graphic to direct the attention of the viewer to a specific point on the page.

Eyes are gateways to the mind, and presentations have to be designed to stimulate the eye. Pictorial information helps the student to process the information. Eyes process images sixty thousand times faster then words (Burmark, 2002), so they have to have context, directly or indirectly, and a relevancy to the point being made.

Points to Remember

- Place your images with care.
- Compel the viewer to follow.

- Use sparingly.
- Use Photoshop or any type of program that allows you to focus this image.
- Set images up to force viewers' eyes onto the page.
- Apparent motion needs to go to most significant point on page. Force viewers' eyes to critical point on the page.
- Use white space to force the learner's eye to a spot or section on a page.
- Visual images have to be of high quality.
- Avoid similar colors, need contrast, primary colors.
- Graphs and charts are good—spreadsheets are deadly.
- Our minds read images sixty thousand times quicker then we read text.

Create a Template for Your Page

Now after you have done all this planning, you are ready to create a template. This should include:

- Course title page template.
- Content template.
- Transition template (when I finish one point giving students indication I am going to another point).
- Resources templates.
- Readings template.

When templates are ready, you will be able to plop them into the place you need them, so the entire course has the same look and feel. Creating templates allows you to pour the ideas in. Another suggestion is to use pre-designed templates that provide you with step-by-step suggestions and a series of layouts you can choose from. In the beginning, this is a good way to start, or you may want to design your own selecting your fonts, colors, and bullets. One last caution before launching your pages: Be sure to test *everything* in several browsers. Then cut and paste your content into your online course.

The Look and Feel of Online Text

An important visual element is the alignment of the text elements and objects — or whether they are really not aligned. If you're sending a message that says "I am purposely not aligning this," then you need to use markers for the key points, not your entire message. Key words have to be easily absorbed. However, you must not draw undue attention from your message with fonts or images and as a result lose the reader–student. Decorative fonts need to be congruent with the content or message. As I stated before, you do not want to create a ransom-note effect by combining too great a variety of font styles, sizes, or colors.

The justification choice you select for your type is very important. Text that is left justified is 30 to 40 percent more readable because we read from left to right. This applies to titles as well. Titles should always be on left rather then center because in a Web format the visual center is not the mathematical center, meaning the title breaks the page into two unequal but pleasing to the eye segments. The best visual center is approximately one-third of the way down the page. This is the place to draw your students' attention for quick analysis. A good rule of thumb is, it is best to put text on the left side and the image on the right side; this style is used by designers for the greatest impact. The preferable line length has text ending in the middle of the page or at a maximum two-thirds of page. Consider using a "soft return" — hold shift key down and press return.

Other Effects

Bullets also help to keep text ordered. The reader's eye tends to gravitate to graphic elements first. On the Web, don't capitalize the first word in a bulleted list unless it is a full sentence. Eliminate anything unnecessary, like articles, adjectives, and verbs.

Use calming colors (e.g., blue) when possible; white and black are the most readable and contrasting colors. "Builds" should still be visible but not a dominant color. A "build" series, often referred to as "builds," is a variation of a bulleted list in which each item is highlighted as discussion progresses. Usually the completed items remain on the visual in a dimmed color, while the current item is highlighted in a brighter color. Use colors to keep the audience focused and provide visual cues that things are moving on with transitions. Use one consistent transition style, like wipe left to right. Well-selected effects have purpose with the message.

Online Demonstrations

Online demonstrations can be an effective device to convey information and to capture audience attention. For the best impact, stand left of screen (stage right) in video demonstrations. This way you become the anchor at the beginning.

Points of Importance

- Edit, edit, and edit some more.
- Streamline.
- Proof for spelling errors or typos.
- Consider getting someone else to edit because you are too close to it.

Evaluation

Once you have established your desired result and created your online environment or presentation, you will want to make sure that you have kept the end in mind while trying to make a complex subject simpler. Import it into your course only after you have refined, refined, refined. Last but not least, evaluate. In figure 3.2, I share an example of how I solicit feedback from my students on my courses. I encourage you to evaluate your end result on these three key points:

- Content
- Technique
- Impact

You have to have all three!

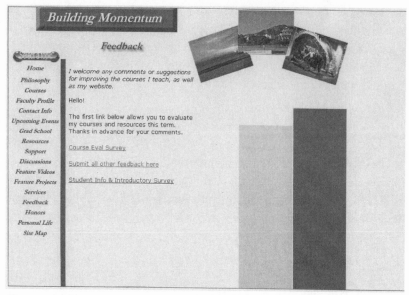

Figure 3.2.   Feedback

CONCLUSIONS

When using Web resources that contain graphics or animation, we can
either help or hinder learners' understanding of material that is presented (Hannafin and Hooper, 1989). With this in mind, we need to use
guidelines that take learning theory into account. Since the computer
screen presents information in a visual format, it is beneficial to recall
the work done by Gestaltists and apply that information to the instructional design of the screens. We can apply the laws of perception to enhance how learners obtain knowledge from the screens. In addition, we
can consider how to create visual "gestalts" for learners when using
graphics and animation. With the increased use of computers for instruction, it is important to move toward the best screen designs for
instruction that we can create.

CHAPTER 4

Communication and Community
Create Online Success

Learning is a social process that occurs through interpersonal interaction within a cooperative context. Individuals, working together,
construct shared understandings and knowledge.

—David Johnson, Roger Johnson, and Karl Smith

CREATING COMMUNITY

Creating an online environment that fosters community and collaboration requires facilitation and nurturing from the instructor. Your community will not run perfectly overnight—you need to give it a little
push to get the ball rolling. As the facilitator, your job is to encourage
the forward movement of conversation that is relevant to the course
work. To help you do this we will provide some guidelines that need to
be made clear to the group from the beginning. The process of setting
expectations for communication consists of:

1. Communication protocol
2. Expected projects
3. Expected requirements within projects
4. Quantity of interaction
5. Method of project turn-in
6. Method for grading
7. Method for peer or instructor feedback
8. Necessity of uniformity for listing times of meetings for Web-
   based courses
9. Course navigation to facilitate easy discovery of resources

Carefully consider the environment as you plan for your students' activities. Allowing for more activity and more options encourages multiple ways of learning. Create new, exciting, and challenging ways of learning for students in your online course. Consider the following questions:

- How will an activity or project impact the culture of community?
- How can the community you establish benefit your students?

Looking in detail at these questions as you design your community, you can give your students a very clear idea of what you want them to accomplish and how they should work together to do it. In this design, it is important to give your students ideas of how they can assist one another. Learning communities attempt to advance collective knowledge to support individual knowledge. In figure 4.1, a model of an ideal virtual learning community is illustrated in this adaptation from Palloff's and Pratt's book *Building Learning Communities in Cyberspace* (1998). The authors maintain that for a virtual learning environment to be effective, priority needs to be given to developing a dynamic sense of community among the group of learners. Their learning occurs from one another, so participation with and the reflection of their peers are essential. Educators need to focus on the learners' self-image and

Figure 4.1.   Diagram of the Components of a Virtual Learning Community (Pratt, 1999)

make them members of the group or club by engaging them in activities they find comprehensible, interesting, and confidence building.

Classroom Communication

In the guidelines of the course, students need to be encouraged to be active participants. Good course attendance will definitely help students' performance. They will feel like they have contributed to the discussion of the community. Ideally, students will begin to connect ideas through group discussion. You will be able to see knowledge as it develops in the community.

With traditional classroom groups, it is possible for only about 35 percent of the participants to converse and have input during an average one-hour, face-to-face discussion. However, online everyone can speak and discuss at the same time. The Internet gives us the opportunity to engage more learners in discussion, an essential learning activity. Discussion (written or verbal) is one method of synthesizing information. Having the ability to actually *say* your idea is empowering in and of itself. Having an instructor or another student comment on your thought in a positive way creates enthusiasm, eagerness to continue, and willingness to comment further. It also helps in forming clarity of thought for the one sharing his or her ideas. Instructors and peers can encourage students in groups to examine issues in ways individuals may not. Many educators agree that online discussions are better than face-to-face discussions for allowing more people to be heard and become active participants in the learning process. The semblance of anonymity allows students who may be more reticent in a face-to-face setting the opportunity to be more active in the dialogue.

Instructors can have students spend a great deal of time discussing alternative strategies with one another in groups and as a whole class. The teacher often participates in these discussions but almost never demonstrates the solutions to problems. The amount of modeling and coaching needed decreases as students' skills increase and as peers and near peers begin to fill in as role models and coaches.

The visual information easily projected using chat tools helps students justify their answers, especially when dealing with abstract concepts. It enhances communication as they make their reasoning visible (e.g., sonic waves and chemical reactions). Classes that have a focus or end product required as a result of the discussion elevate the dialogue to a level of mapping an understanding of the concepts being presented. These types of discussions allow students to suggest solutions and then see simulations of the effects of their solutions within the group.

Factors in Developing Online Community

We feel that the initial face-to-face meeting is key in the development of the online community. The bond that is established is one that cannot be created by just coming together online. The underlying group connection that is formed at the initial meeting sets the tone in the online community. At this time, members of the group will develop strong reciprocal ties, personal access to other members bonding on a non-academic level, and using real names to create a familiar form of communicating that will follow the group into synchronous and asynchronous environments. Through days of shared team projects, the group work and feedback that will be required over the coming months will begin to take shape. Support groups will form.

Electronic communication can be a cold medium. However, people have invented ways to be quite expressive, and friendships will be formed. People will find those with whom they share a common bond, gravitating to those they want to learn from and deciding that there will be people whom they choose not to interact with. Students will meet others who they might consider experts in their own field, and a teacher–student relationship will be formed among members of the group. The true colors of group members will, without a doubt, come out. Who knows what, who is willing to show others what they know, and who will need their hand held, all become very apparent in the course of just a few days. People will emerge as leaders in the group. You will have one or two students that seem to influence or moderate the group as a whole. Cliques will form and you will watch personalities gravitate both in person and online. You may find a varying age range among group members or certain career paths lead some to become mentors for their younger cohort mates. You may see persons settle into groups by age or career path. People who are new to a career or lacking specific life experiences will find mentors and drink deeply from the knowledge they have brought to the class. In this way, the new community is strengthened and nourishes its own members.

With a strong commitment from facilitators for the face-to-face discussion and from the members of the program, an enormous amount can be accomplished in a very short period of time. Technical skills required for being a part of an online community are developed everyday, but first impressions hold for a lifetime. It is essential that the face-to-face facilitators know that they will be expected to have a hand in each members' impression of the program and of the other members. It is important that the facilitators take the job very seriously, are organized, and have a clear plan for the encounter to ensure all goes smoothly. This is an opportunity for honest reflection on the part of program facilitators. There is a real difference between behind-the-scenes activity and behind-the-scenes chaos. I think the difference is obvious even to the uninitiated. Behind-the-scenes plans produce confident-looking facilitators and, consequently, confident participants. Although they will not be giving away a lot of information to the group, the behind-the-scenes activity will be goal orientated and group orientated. This will not be what the group sees; as the point is for each member to construct his or her own experience without feeling that they are a part of someone else's agenda. When people run something there is always a tacit understanding that there is an "agenda"; the question is, is the agenda honest, obvious, and in line with my personal agenda? The agenda of creating a learning community can be this honest; the students should be able to construct their own experience within the stated agenda of the practicing facilitators. This honesty of agenda should help create an open culture.

To build a culture rather than just support a community, careful reflection about what kind of culture you want to create is needed well in advance. You will find that participation, as a peer, will set the tone for openness and thoughtful feedback among the group, as well as establish a trust between you, as the facilitator, and the students.

Techniques for Community

Without specific characteristics of community in mind, it will be very difficult to develop techniques to reach the end that you envision. Problems and personality conflicts will arise among group members.

You will need to have an initial idea how you hope that the group will handle issues that will arise throughout the length of the course or program. It is important to encourage the group to discuss problem-solving strategies, reminding the group they might be better off choosing to form a committee to solve the problem and to assign group facilitators. Most absolute guidelines have a tendency to fall by the wayside; instead, a more effective problem-solving strategy for the group might be to implement incremental problem-solving skills for the members using the steps in the process below:

- Brainstorming
- Research
- Negotiation
- Drafting
- Editing
- Reflecting

It is important that the group members feel comfortable approaching one another with anything, that they can feel confident that their opinions will be respected even if they are not the opinions of the majority. A key aspect of developing your community is establishing the importance of respect and trust. Help the group understand that not everyone will agree all the time, and mistakes will be made in following the group norms, but respect is key to maintaining a virtually perfect world. Make it clear that as the instructor, you will need to be made aware if there is a larger issue in the group that cannot be resolved, but, for the most part, the instructor is not and will not be a policeman, and the group is responsible for constant, effective, and respectful communication. Learning in a group is an experience that allows you to become more open–minded, from sharing ideas with others, than a one-sided opinion from self-taught learners. Respect can be exhibited by learning to understand viewpoints with which you do not agree.

Techniques for Assigning Groups

Random methods of organizing students, such as alphabetically, for activities designed for the purpose of "getting to know one another" work best. They do not allow for the formation of cliques or people with prior friendship to group together. One way to organize students for projects is to have them select a group by subspecialty, type of project, or book group for the occasions when you have optional reading choices.

Example: Instructions for Optional Book Groups

This week:

1. Choose one of the following books and get into groups to discuss one of the following:
   • Web Learning Fieldbook: "Using the WWW to Build Workplace Environments" http://www.pfeiffer.com/beer.html
   • "Points of Viewing, Children's Thinking" http://www.pointsof viewing.com (case studies and methodology describing the process of observing thinking in constructivists classrooms)

2. For whatever book you choose, view the companion Web site and read the book prior to meeting.

Next week:

1. Meet in your optional book group in online classroom for discussion.
2. Discuss how the book relates to your practice and impacts learning.
3. Post the group members, a short summary, insights, and the transcript afterward.

Contact me if you have any questions.

Prof. X

In this way, students are in a group based on their mutual interest in the topic, and this heightens motivation. For classes where students are in the same general area, some groups are formed on a geographical basis. Then they can meet face to face or even have small-group meetings. For some purposes, you, as the teacher, want to purposefully mix students in groups to balance technological skills, leadership ability, subject-matter expertise, and diversity. Do this based on firsthand knowledge of your students though, not on a Profiler, which can be in-accurate. You might combine some experienced students with inexpe-rienced ones. Create online environments that allow students to work in a variety of small groups, if possible, for some projects for an ex-tended period of time. Teachers have reported success with all of the above methods. You have a variety of options depending on your dis-cipline and situation.

Motivational Techniques

To develop an understanding of the characteristics of his or her on-line students, it is recommended that the instructor participate in some kind of "icebreaker" activities alongside the students. In your commu-nity, this will help to create a warm, inviting course environment. Par-ticipation in these activities will show you as a real person, a mentor, a friend, a confidant, and not just the "instructor." These activities should occur before and during any face-to-face meeting for the group. If for some reason the group does not seem as connected as you might have hoped, some of these activities could be incorporated into the distance-learning experience and shared in the asynchronous or synchronous en-vironment.

Ask students to begin with introductions and state their name, school, where they grew up, and a memorable (positive) learning ex-perience that influenced them. As the instructor, you could describe one of the most stimulating Web-based learning experiences you have par-ticipated in. An agenda might include introductions among participants and leaders, course overview, philosophy, maybe a description in slide-show or video format for illustration, personal survey of Web tools, learning styles or leadership skills, featured sites, resources, tools, and phone numbers.

In many face-to-face classes, I take time during the first class session to explore "assumptions" about learning (and teaching). Most of the di-alogue has centered around the ideas on the subject of "traditional teaching." I then have used these ideas and others to "reorient" my stu-dents toward a much more active learning, participative learning, and community-building approach for face-to-face. I see extending this dialogue and reshaping it a bit for the orientation for online or blended classes.

Consider posting throughout the course on class days a "live" Web shot that one can see on those days' "Welcome" page. Any time during those days, I can take another photo, and it gets automatically posted in my online office or to the course classroom or Web site. It could be a picture of the instructor demonstrating something. There is a little camera that sits on (or near) the instructor's computer and software on the computer. Whenever I take a shot, I click on the mouse and take a photo. I have it "programmed" so that the picture automatically is posted in the online classroom and in my virtual office. Figures 4.2 and 4.3 are examples of what appears on my course site and virtual office. The Web-cam idea can be used for spicing up and personalizing the site. There, on the screen, is the instructor, welcoming the student. This can be a nice way of encouraging, energizing, and communicating. This is a fun idea and increasingly easy to do.

Figure 4.2. *Welcome*

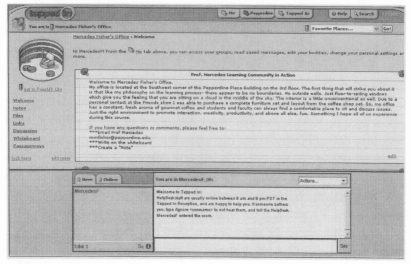

Figure 4.3.   *Tapped In Office*

Social Icebreakers

Create a supportive community that extends the class out to students and their interests, ideas, and thoughts. Communication from you must be clear, precise, and most importantly open-ended. Remember that the instructor acts as a moderator rather than the sole source of information. Icebreakers are a fun way to begin developing a sense of community in your online classes. It can be challenging to get students to interact asynchronously, and icebreakers give them a chance to get to know one another in a non-threatening manner. Course members need to get acquainted, and the instructor creates this comfort level through safe activities and social icebreakers and by encouraging students to risk sharing their opinions with one other—all done in a climate that establishes tolerance and acceptance of different communication styles and creates mutual respect and trust among students. The first few weeks can lay the groundwork for group collaboration later in class.

We have listed some activities below that might assist in effective group or team building. These "getting to know one another" icebreakers have proven effective in group settings for forming relationships that will last throughout the length of the program and beyond. Icebreakers are most helpful for all learning styles when they connect students to the topic as well as to one another. They reduce isolation and are a key factor in connecting people and content. Some of these icebreakers can be used in the initial face-to-face meeting, and others can be adapted for use online.

- Scavenger hunt/Internet hunt. Find information on Web or around class site.
- Two truths, one lie. List three items, and the class votes on which one is a lie.
- Coffeehouse. Everyone posts two or three expectations, and the instructor summarizes and comments on how they may be met.
- Seven nouns activity. Introduce yourself using seven nouns and explain why you chose each noun.
- Peer interviews. Share introductions of one another and/or find or create a Web object inspired by your peer and share it with the larger class and why you made your decision.
- Field definition activity. Students interview someone working in the field—via email if necessary. As a class, pool interview results and develop a description of what it means to be a professional in the field.
- Round robin. Select a topic, respond to it, and pass the answer to the next person in the group; keep passing until everyone contributes or ideas are exhausted. Summarize or report findings.
- Cartoon. Find a Web site that has cartoons and have students link their introductions or stories to a particular cartoon URL. Storytelling is a good way to communicate.
- Favorite or most recent book, movie, breakfast cereal, dessert, condiment. . . . Have students answer questions such as "If you could have only one [fill in the blank] the rest of your life what would it be and why? While talking about movies, people start reciting funny and/or memorable lines, and their personalities peek through.
- Share two books that made a difference in your life and why.
- Remind students of the song "Itsy Bitsy Spider" and ask them to compare it with their careers. Encourage them to talk about failures; this puts everyone on an even approach as they see that failures are okay.

- Favorite quotation. Choose a quotation and discuss why it is a favorite.
- Look at the profiles of people in your cooperative group or team. In particular, read their "favorite quotation" and then share a comment about the quotations with the other members of your cooperative group. This will give you practice holding a discussion with your group members.
- Human knot. Students clasp one another's hands in the center of a circle. To untangle themselves, they must work together.
- Train wreck–community shuffle. Give students one question. All who can answer it run to change to another open seat. Students cannot stay in their seats each time if their response is "yes" to the question.
- Flip card with an animal on one side, two characteristics that relate on the other, neighbor seated next to participant guesses what animal and gives rationale—see if perceptions of others of us match our own.
- Opening and closing ceremony. Provide an opportunity for all class participants (sitting in a circle) to express what they are feeling or learned in the group.

Another option is to collect student background information on a form from your Web site. An example of this type of form is shown in figure 4.4.

Community-building Activities

At your initial face-to-face meeting it is important to do some community-building activities to enable students to work together for the first time and get a feel for the personalities that exist within the group. At Pepperdine, we like to allocate four to five days for the first face-to-face meeting that we call VirtCamp. As illustrated in figure 4.5, the community is always expanding. Each new cohort is mentored not only by faculty and staff but by alumni with an interest in the ongoing success of the community. The notion of "Community of Practice" is broader from day one of VirtCamp. This should extend to all students past and present, all faculty, and guest speakers. In my opinion, a community of practice is inclusive. You can love your family and welcome neighbors as well.

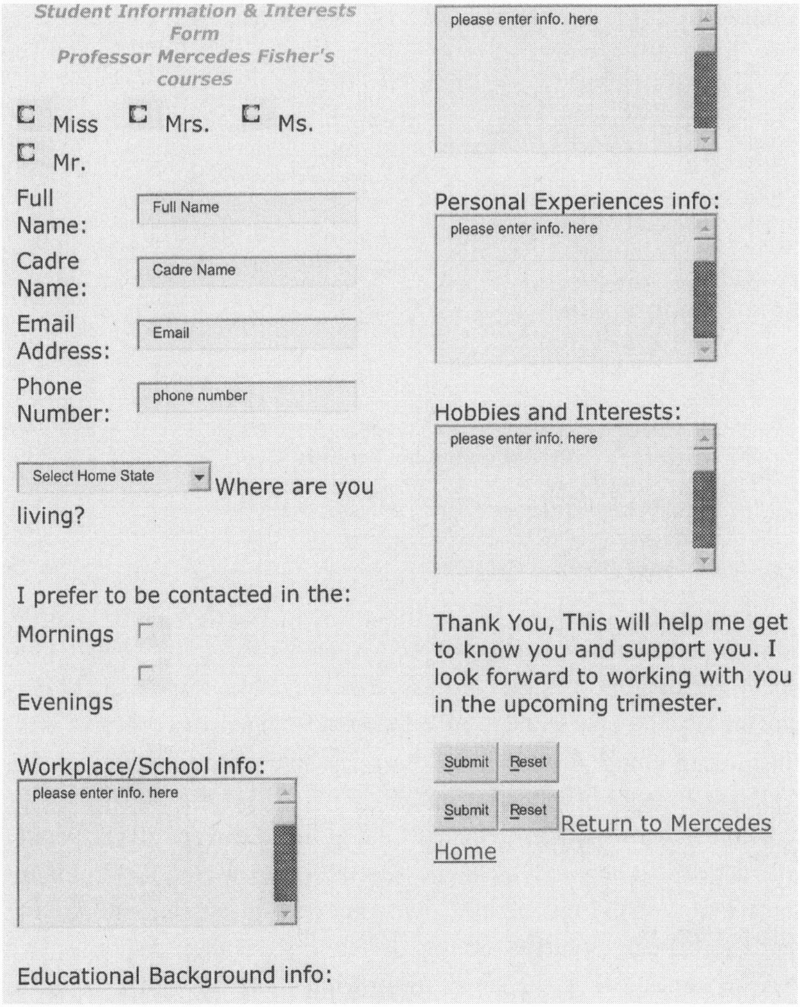

Student Information & Interests Form
Professor Mercedes Fisher's courses

☐ Miss   ☐ Mrs.   ☐ Ms.
☐ Mr.

Full Name: [Full Name]

Cadre Name: [Cadre Name]

Email Address: [Email]

Phone Number: [phone number]

[Select Home State ▼] Where are you living?

I prefer to be contacted in the:

Mornings ☐

☐
Evenings

Workplace/School info:
[please enter info. here]

Educational Background info:

[please enter info. here]

Personal Experiences info:
[please enter info. here]

Hobbies and Interests:
[please enter info. here]

Thank You, This will help me get to know you and support you. I look forward to working with you in the upcoming trimester.

[Submit] [Reset]

[Submit] [Reset] Return to Mercedes Home

Figure 4.4.   *Information and Interests Form*

At VirtCamp the students are asked to do open-ended tasks in groups that allow the students to interact with one another and get a feel for the program they are about to enter. Two of our favorite activities are a problem-solving challenge using Lego bricks and a group sharing activity based on the *Iron Chef* cooking show.

In this activity, students are grouped randomly and given a project using Lego bricks and an RCX Yellowbrick that they have to program using Logo software. Students are then required to work together, without

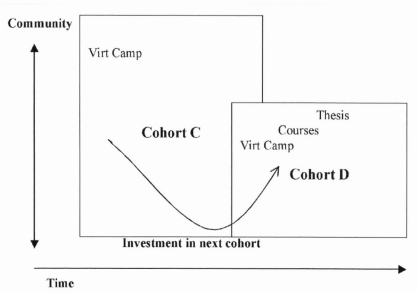

Figure 4.5.   *Iterative Communities*

being given a lot of structure or specific guidelines besides being told to document and reflect on the "process" they undertake. It is about the journey the students take, going from a group of strangers to a cohesive well-functioning group. It is in this activity that many roles are defined and people's strengths become apparent.

In the *Iron Chef* activity, students are grouped and are given specific instructions on how to chop some vegetables. However, it is in the interpretation of the instructions that some real discussion and talking starts to happen. Students are then asked to share their responses to a series of questions in the small group while working with the vegetables, and then to look at other groups' end products and finally to come back as a whole group to discuss what they have learned and to make meaning out of the task. This activity attempts to find some common connection among people who might have extremely different backgrounds and outlooks on life but have committed to sharing an experience together in this online program. The heart of the success of both of these tasks is that they require production of something that no one person in the group is already immediately familiar with. In other words, leaders, researchers, coaches, and cheerleaders all emerge in a vacuum of the needed technical skills, and so a whole-group experience is likely to emerge. The *Iron Chef* activity begins to fall flat if one member of the group, in fact, is a chef and truly knows how to chiffonade, just as the Lego activity falls flat in the face of a real "Yellowbrick" maven. I think it is necessary to create new activities based on your audience.

Group Size

The size of the group definitely makes a difference. At Pepperdine, we limit the size of each group. Henry and Rigault have the opinion that at least fifteen persons will be needed in order to ensure a minimum of messages. We have found in our online program that about twenty-five students works best as far as student and instructor satisfaction. Large groups are better suited for conferences or discussions that aim to explore and collect information; small groups of three to five are more effective in joint projects in order to facilitate coordination. Many of our students are still comparing their online course to a face-to-face class, and they are craving individual attention from the instructor. Online courses *can* be effective, even in large numbers, if they are properly designed and moderated, even though a large group is not an ideal situation.

Classes are offered to groups at two different meeting times to accommodate the various student locations. Each synchronous discussion group includes approximately eight to ten students in each session. For example, classes could be offered at 6:30 A.M. and 7:30 P.M. We encourage students to attend only one session of each class each week in the synchronous environments so that the groups are not too big and everyone has a voice. As students meet in their virtual classroom, the size will often dictate how the class is conducted. For example, if more than twelve people attend the same session, the instructor may have the groups break up into smaller groups of two or three. Then the groups can meet in separate virtual rooms to discuss questions or topics presented. Later, everyone gets back together as a whole for a final wrap-up of the small-group meetings. This allows the larger group to reassemble and have a shared focus.

Limiting group size is done not to restrict ideas but to allow room for them to flow. It is important to have a group large enough so that thoughts will be diverse but small enough for all members to be heard. The small-group size will also foster playful interaction among the members. A general rule as to how many students should be in an online class, most of the time, should be determined by the subject matter and/or activities needed to communicate the concepts effectively. There seems to be tremendous variety in online goals and audiences.

Most online research supports a smaller class size and states that it takes much longer to develop and facilitate an online course because of the increased interaction that is required for online education to "work." We need to remember that online education is a new medium to deliver quality education and that one size does not fit all. Most colleges would not create generalized rules for all subject areas, so that strategy should also not occur with online courses. Instead, it should be tailored to the subject.

STRATEGIES FOR SUCCESSFUL ONLINE LEARNING

Online learning is new. High drop-out rates in Web-based classes in both education and business are common. According to the *Chronicle of Higher Education* fewer than 50 percent of distance-education students finish their courses. Motorlola University found that a significant gap existed between the number of employees who register for online courses and the number who actually complete them, with 70 percent of online learners dropping out (Jackson 2001). However, we are already discovering ways to improve the practice of online learning. About 50 percent of online learners don't complete a course, says Eric Parks, founder of ASK International, a training and research development firm in Fair Oaks, California. Parks's research is based on employee training in the for-profit sector, but it points to problems and barriers for all online learners, regardless of the situation or setting. However, we are already discovering ways to improve the practice of online learning, as outlined in this book.

In a session at the national Online Learning conference, session participants brainstormed ways to improve online learning to make it work. Those ideas fell into four categories:

1. Orienting online learners before course starts.
2. Providing online learners with information on software and hardware.
3. Giving support, help, and encouragement to online learners.
4. Improving the design of the online course.

Orientation

It is strongly advised to have a face-to-face kick-off meeting or orientation upon acceptance to the program. In the Pepperdine model, this initial meeting, along with two other face-to-face gatherings, is a required component of the program. The first time the group meets is a site visit and a chance to get acquainted; the second time is about midway through the course, when they demonstrate some proficiency and can be evaluated by one another as well as by an outside expert. The third time is toward the end of the course, when they present an independent project that they have worked on throughout the program.

We feel the initial meeting works well in getting everyone acquainted with one another and in discussing his or her role in this community and for future projects. This meeting is a time when students should become familiar with the tools that they will be using. Figure 4.6 is a sample VirtCamp schedule to help you visualize how the day's activities are laid out. Many tools become obsolete, so, as you will see, we do not cover specific tools here. This is a good time for the facilitators of the course to get a feel for who knows what in terms of technological skill for the current tools standards in their program. It is important to stress that these tools are all things that can be learned. There will be no one in the community who will not be able to function. The learning curve here will cause some visible stress and frustration among certain members of the group. Facilitators of this kick-off meeting will need to underscore the importance of keeping an open mind. Encourage members of the group to be teachers, and help those who seem to struggle. It is through this initial struggle that one enters the culture of the community. This is a time where people connect with the cohort. Personal relationships are formed and learning circles are created. We feel that the success of the Pepperdine online model is due to both the constant communication and the trust that is

3:15 PM	3:30 PM	Bio Break, with Refreshments
3:30 PM	4:30 PM	Lego/Logo and/or Digital Movie Lab Time
4:30 AM	4:45 PM	Community Building: Trainwreck
4:45 PM	5:15 PM	staff - Server Issues
5:15 PM	6:00 PM	Reflection and Community Circle - Discuss Dinner Together
Friday (VI - 7/19, VII - 7/26)		
8:30 AM	9:00 AM	Continental Breakfast
9:00 AM	10:00 AM	ED 640/641 Professors will hold class with their cohort
10:00 AM	10:15 AM	Bio Break
10:15 AM	11:15 AM	PepXpress
11:15 AM	12:15 PM	An Online Class Experience: TI - Discussion on Reading, or Idea sharing for Lego
12:15 PM	1:15 PM	Lunch Break-On Your Own
1:15 PM	2:15 PM	Community Building: Bridge Building
2:15 PM	2:30 PM	Bio Break, with Refreshments
2:30 PM	4:30 PM	ED 640/641 Lab Time: Lego/Logo and/or Digital Movie
4:30 PM	5:00 PM	Group Name announcements/ Cross Cohort Meeting Info.
5:00 PM	5:30 PM	Reflection and Community Circle
Saturday (VI - 7/20, VII - 7/27)		
8:30 AM	9:00 AM	Continental Breakfast
9:00 AM	10:30 AM	Final Lego/Logo Session (Show and Tell Setup)
10:30 AM	10:45 AM	Bio Break
10:45 AM	12:15 PM	Lab Time-Lego/Logo Show and tell
12:15 PM	1:15 PM	Lunch Break - *Pizza on Pepperdine*
1:15 PM	2:45 PM	Housekeeping and Ongoing Support Fall Courses and Registration; CSCL; Mid-Point Meeting; Contacting Staff; Shirt Distribution; collectives Confirm Address/E-Mail/Phone#/Listserv exchange
2:45 PM	3:00 PM	Bio Break, with Refreshments
3:00 PM	3:30 PM	Q & A with Past OMAET Graduates
3:30 PM	4:00 PM	Community Building Cadre - Note on the back activity
4:00 PM	4:30 PM	Reflection and Community Circle (Collective)

Figure 4.6.   *Orientation Meeting Schedule*

developed during the first face-to-face meeting. We encourage you to use such meetings in any of the following ways:

- Tell online learners what to expect before the course starts.
- Consider creating an online tutorial that students must visit before enrolling in an online class, as some institutions already require. Others are dispersing CD-ROMs with simulations of an online course. This sets the pace early on for students to aspire to meet. CD-ROMs are good supplements to courses because students can see materials without having to dial up or connect to a network.
- Have student training on how to learn online.
- Encourage online learners to find or create a learning space where they will not be interrupted.

- Explain the more efficient uses of synchronous and asynchronous discussions.
- Provide support, help, and encouragement to online learners.
- Have mentors available for content support.
- Provide personal information of other participants in the online course.

Working in a virtual group is challenging! Students have their own priorities, and they don't necessarily match your own; however, you work through it and, for the most part, it is hard work and stimulating. Using the right mix of both to keep students motivated will provide for a meaningful and successful learning community.

Software and Hardware Information

It is likely that not all members of your course are familiar with the software you will be using. It is helpful to the course experience to provide online learners with information on software and hardware related to the online course. You might want to work this into your initial face-to-face orientation. Here are some tips to remember:

- Label what browser and access speed works best for the online course.
- Have your information technology (IT) department or technical people preload plug-ins before the course starts. Test all software and plug-ins first.
- Have a help desk with phone number for learners to call if they have any problems.
- Offer troubleshooting basics to students:
  - Reboot. Solves over half of all problems.
  - Try it again. The action not working.
  - Wait. Too many people may be trying to access the same resources from the host server at the same time. Take the dog for a walk, have a beverage, or relax.
  - Check ISP for congestion, storm, and maintenance problems.
  - Call your tech support.

Support and Encouragement

Support and encouragement are key to helping your students achieve their goals in your course. Provide plenty of timely and narrative feedback. Also, be readily available to answer questions. As an instructor, you should

- Give quick, helpful, and insightful feedback for assignments and projects.
- Send personal emails to answer concerns.
- Respond to message board and threaded discussion postings frequently. This is the best way to keep a discussion moving and well read; students love reading how you respond to other students!

Techniques to Improve Course Design

Many instructors choose to prepare the entire online course before the date the course starts, which is commonly referred to as "front loading"—all modules are up and running by the first day of the course. Often in classes, something will arise during the course that needs or warrants attention, though it was not in the original plan. By surveying students, instructors can get feedback from students whenever they want (preferably before the end of term!) and use this feedback to modify areas of the course that may not be working for that particular class of students. Also, note that surveys do not have to be formal instruments; they can be "how's it going?" posts in the threaded discussion area, as you are trying to achieve feedback in any form. Instructors need to be willing to let the course evolve with the students' needs and interests related to the content. The students can be divided into subgroups and special-interest groups, also. Then, other students interested in the same focus can post messages and share thoughts. Techniques for addressing topics that arise in class may include:

- Providing links to external Web-based content for students to read and explore that address the new topic.
- Discussing it online.

- Turning it into a project that ends with the student's research, tutorials, simulations, individual case studies, interactive flashcards, or group project, such as a group PowerPoint presentation, group Web site, a group role play, a group debate, a group paper or essay, or a group virtual tour.
- Anticipate a couple of new areas and prepare optional content in case the topic arises.
- Change discussion strategies as the course progresses based on student needs. What works for one class of students may not work for another, so be flexible.

Depending on course activities, most of the course may be online, but some topics or discussions are unveiled at the date of the activity so that students stay within a time limit for that piece. This encourages students to collaborate and communicate about the topic at hand instead of rushing ahead. An additional option is to make course materials available on a week-by-week basis. This may be a drawback for some who feel it interferes with a student's own pace. On the other hand, some faculties are concerned about overwhelming the students with all the course material all at once.

Creating Interaction

Whether a course is online or face-to-face (or some of both), three types of interactions are relevant to course design:

1. Student-to-content interaction.
2. Student-to-student interaction.
3. Student-to-instructor/facilitator interaction.

Student-to-Content Interaction

Here, we can focus in on the student's ability to interact with the course material. If we focus on the student's ability to demonstrate that he or she understands the concepts, can articulate a meaningful option about the ideas, or even ask a relevant question about the material, we might be able to assess whether or not the student has sufficiently "interacted" with the content.

In an online setting, how does one determine what amount of interactivity between learners and content is required? It is up to each individual teacher to determine based on subject matter and student needs.

Student-to-Student Interaction

Effective use of peer support has been identified by Salomon (1991) as "distributed cognition." Rather than placing an equal and separate cognitive load on each student, peer support can distribute the load, freeing up the instructor. When students approach the instructor with general-knowledge questions, the instructor can direct them to peers that the instructor, having monitored the individual progress and understanding of each student, knew could help. Subsequently, the instructor was free to continue monitoring the class and deal with more difficult questions and issues. Learning is a matter of enculturation; your identity evolves through access to knowledge or expertise in use around you and through interaction with objects and people (Lave and Wenger, 1991; Wenger, 1998).

On the first day of class, it is often difficult to make conversation with the bright shiny faces (computer icons) around you, and yet you crave contact with people who have put themselves in the same situation as you. The instructor can immediately facilitate conversation by utilizing community-building activities (see section on icebreakers) and modeling desired performance.

- Encourage students to answer their classmates' questions.
- Consider using Instant Messenger as a way for students to connect with one another synchronously. Publish a username list on the course site for easy reference.
- Jumpstart the participation by asking someone to comment on another's work, and then allow for a rebuttal by the originator of such work. Be prepared for potential rules for these situations, like if the first student never answers the questions. Recognition among their peers works most of the time.
- Create small groups of four to five students. For the first three weeks, the students are required to post individual responses on the discussion board. This provided time allows for students to get

to know who is in their group. After the third week, assign group activities. They will work together better and might even initiate group chats in the chat room as they develop their topics.

Student–to–Instructor Interaction

When designing an online course, think about the first day of your typical face-to-face class. As you are introducing yourself and the course syllabus, have you noticed the blank stares you get, the puzzled look on some of the faces? Students are, in essence, asking a question. What do you expect from me in this course? The same thing occurs the first day online and is compounded by the lack of nonverbal cues.

- Be available. Many instructors have office hours online in a chat or meeting tool. Post these office hours and be prepared for students to take advantage of them. Remind students that you are available at certain times and look forward to talking with them.
- Respond quickly. Most instructors try to answer email within seventy-two hours.
- Anticipate questions and provide answers in a "frequently asked questions" page.
- Create a welcome page with things like instructor picture, contact info, favorite quotation, and teaching philosophy.
- Send welcome letters or email to your students, welcoming them to your course and expressing your excitement at working with them.
- Create a unique signature for yourself on purpose. Personalize icons when possible.
- Address students by their first name or preferred nickname if they have asked for it.
- Encourage the students to make public and personal acknowledgements of birthdays, anniversaries, and celebrations. Add your own personal sentiments to your students.

Also, the first two to three weeks are essential periods for online classes. Instructors must stay in close contact with students during this time. Students who do not sign on the first week need to have some form of contact. I usually call since the absence of contact may mean technical problems. Although it is important to have some face-to-face interaction, it is not essential.

The following is an example of student-to-teacher interaction in the form of an email as a result of the synchronous discussion shown in figure 2.6 in chapter 2. This shows the open relationship between the student and the teacher and how it is not an authoritarian relationship but more of a collaborative one. One issue we have in a program based upon a notion of learning as transformation (rather than transmission) is how to assess it—how to demonstrate' student learning. The community of practice model tells us that people's learning is evident in the shift in their identity/role/participation in their practice. Testimonials like this seem to indicate that.

(1) I'm wrapping up my workplace case study, I think you'll dig it, just having some people at work go over it with me, it's become an integral ARP piece as well, more data and evidence. I shifted from my original proposal as posted in NGs, and completely followed your rubric and syllabus (well, I loosely let it guide me I mean—I mean, it helped me design my case study approach), it's amazing how much you can get out of re-reading the syllabus once you have more knowledge in a course—it's true that the light just starts turning on . . . a-ha . . . click . . . a-ha . . . click . . .

(2) On the reform proposal project, I'd love it if you could skim this tranny attached below, for the first time I really felt like I was teaching online, it was really cool—however, I'd feel really bad if I was leading my team in the wrong direction here, not that designing our own understanding could necessarily be the wrong direction (and you know how I'm adjusting to narratives and away from grades, well, you know what I mean).

I feel clear and confident of my understanding of this assignment: to me, a proposal is a plan and reform is change, so I constructed—make a plan of change for our technology case studies. That's what I impressed on to my team. And I think I see what you're doing here, and how this ties into the leadership/mentoring class, and into our ARP . . . and dare I say onto next trimester and beyond when we all have to get ready to take this new knowledge base and go out there and fly!

Am I close here—I feel like this project is a fore-shadow of kicking us out of the nest. This reform proposal and leadership knowledge should inspire us to make us actually do it! I feel that! Making us leaders of

learning and technology! Maybe pulling out one of our grad school projects next year and actually doing it—for real. And we have real data from
our case studies and our workplace study and our ARPs . . . click . . . a-ha
. . . click . . . and we know how to design and shape learning environments,
plan—complete—and pitch technology reform proposals, foster communities of practice, become technology leaders and proponents of change at
work and give back through mentoring . . . being life long learners . . . and,
we'll, I don't mean to make this a book here . . . just a brief testimonial
;-)- This is evidence of how I am learning!
    Thanks

Using Simulations

I have always been a proponent of a live virtual lab program, but resources, combined with recent technological advances in simulation
tools (which make them take much less time to create than in the past),
are making us reconsider the potential effectiveness of simulations,
which sometimes may be even more effective than virtual labs. The
simulations can provide some immediate mentoring, in contrast to
the live virtual labs, which have no instant mentoring capabilities. Un-
fortunately, most courses, to date, have only been able to provide distant learners with "sit and watch" canned software demonstrations
(passive viewing)—not a tremendously effective way to learn. We focus on increasing knowledge and retention by providing a means for
our distant students to actively participate in learning through software
simulations, which provide instant feedback, coaching, and, more importantly, greater retention of knowledge. Interactive simulations allow
the online learner to become an active participant in controlling or manipulating the concepts and ideas they are learning about. Interactive
simulations can be integrated into your course in purposeful ways.
    Simulations are an example of the incredible potential for enhanced
learning online. As with Kathy Konicek, learning technology consultant, Department of Information Technology, University of Wisconsin–Madison, we have found this helpful. The *interactive simulations*
provide varying levels of interactivity for the student. It should be noted
that some interactive simulations may work better with a broadband
(e.g., cable, DSL) connection and some may require a plug-in. Be sure
to give the student links to site where they can acquire any necessary

tools to make the simulations work. One such example, Howard Hughes Medical Institute, www.biointeractive.org, includes a virtual cardiology lab, bacterial ID lab, animations, virtual tours, and Web videos that can be used in courses.

Using Multimedia

Multimedia components can enhance the learning experience for students by appealing to different learning styles and demonstrating in ways that simple text cannot. Type, duration, and quality are key factors when deciding to use animation, video clips, interactive quizzes, audio files, or other media types. Multimedia should complement, not repeat, the text in the course readings.

The disadvantages of using multimedia objects are the large file sizes, increased bandwidth requirements, and long download times. Congested data lines, inadequate connection speeds, and server issues can all restrict access to media files. One alternative solution is to create a CD containing media files and other resources (Diaz, 2002). This allows the students to access the interactive multimedia applications and avoid having to worry about connection issues. Using even simple or small multimedia components now seem like a good idea; bandwidth technical issues will go away soon, and online instructors should be prepared to incorporate these new medias as they become ubiquitous.

Techniques for Individual Learning

In the course of one's individual learning, reflection will show growth and the degree of learning. As the instructor, you will need to find ways above and beyond the asynchronous environment to be able to promote growth and reflection as an excellent insight into one's learning. Encourage the use of online journals, databases, and interest groups where you will be able to check in on the personal, day-to-day happenings of your students. These areas will have a different tone because individuals will be reflecting on their own experiences and interacting with people who may or may not be from their academic environment. You will be able to see if members of the group are applying what the group is learning at individual and personal levels to how they communicate with others.

- Personal journals. These often focus on course concepts, experiences, and readings.
- Internships.
- Action/research project, clinical, or portfolio.
- Authentic data analysis. TimeWeb tools help students visualize, analyze, interpret, and explore space–time dimensions.
- Apprenticeships.
- Reaction papers, postings, or essays that the instructor usually prompts with a dilemma or scenario.
- Case-based laboratories.
- Virtual field trips and tours related to content.
- Socio-cultural field trips. Instructors developed a virtual mediation pond, cabin in the woods, hot tub, and class experience at the top of Mount Rainier, where we went when stressed. It seems weird, but we could actually "feel" a sense of relaxation when we went there as a class and then we could address concepts again more productively.
- Live cameras. Find a current place of study and take a "live tour." Students can see in real time the geographical area they are currently investigating. Find sites prior to working on the case.
- Historical sound clips. Download famous speeches, meeting presentations, and conference speeches.
- Cooperative challenge. Students work together to meet a challenge or solve a problem.
- Survey. Students create a survey on the Web using one of the many free online survey tools to find out and collect information for analysis and study.
- Simulations on the Web. These require students to use their imagination to re-create an event or process. Also, point students to sites that offer simulations such as frog dissections and archeological digs.
- Mentors. Students are paired via email with experts and others of influence in the field they are studying.
- Key pals. Students may, for example, peer critique course assignments. Students participate in communication with another student.

Be sure to structure communication by providing goals other than socialization.

- Multimedia. Use the Web to create multimedia demonstrations for the course.
- Multiple modes of delivery and/or teaching style to the community. Use video streaming, audio streaming, and guest speakers.
- Learning contracts. These allow students to look at a rubric with three to four levels and the activities and assignments associated with each level, and then they decide what they are going to do beforehand to earn a grade (e.g., A, B, C, etc.).

Teaching with Groups

Make some class time available for group work.

- Include a substantial component in the grading system for the group performance so students can see merit and motivation for participation.
- Have both an individual and a group grade.
- Examples: Checklist for each group member that contains helpful insights and suggestions for peer evaluations or complete chart and questions, group vote and rationale for point of view, thorough discussion in small group, participation, etiquette, and preparation and outside research.
- Foster sharing of peer knowledge, questions and expertise.
- Provide immediate feedback.
- Privately, via email or in a chat session, ask non-contributing group members to participate.
- Give them opportunities to make decisions.
- Listen in on group discussions and offer advice when appropriate with leadership and direction to help students apply, analyze, and synthesize content.
- Help them set realistic goals.
- Have students negotiate a group contract for decision-making norms, communication, and conflict-resolution participation.
- Explain why group work is key to the learning process in this type of environment.

- Divide into small groups. Usually three to five students work within a predetermined time limit to answer questions. Our students work in teams a lot. Each team has a private discussion board and a way to share files over the Internet. They use these tools to work on team projects. Often they present their projects as Word documents, but they have also made Web pages and Power Point presentations (both with and without narration). The teams submit their projects, and we put them on a Web server. The teams often then critique the projects on a discussion board.
- Alternative jigsaw techniques. Students can be grouped via a jigsaw pattern, where students are put into numerical groups of perhaps five students. Each student in each group is given a letter from A to E. All the A's (one student from each numerical group) then get together and discuss parts of the assignment. Each letter group works on a different part of the assignment or questions and then takes this work back to their numerical group. This way breaks up the workload and allows each student in the group the chance to peer teach his or her part of the assignment to his or her group.
- Seminars. Read before going online.
- Webinar. Webinar is like a seminar on the Web set up so that scheduled Web meetings can discuss findings and research.
- Tutorials. In some tutorials, students work together with real data so they are exposed to real-life experiences. For example, one instructor is using the Web for the first time in a course on environmental and social change. One of the instructor's challenges has been to help the students learn how to evaluate the movement's origins. Last week they reviewed two sites that are activist sites for farming. Without any explanation, the students could see the dramatic differences in the substantive nature of one site and the superficial, inflammatory nature of the other. They were able to draw conclusions and apply this to other experiences—Web or not.
- Large-group discussions.
- Small-group discussions.
- Forums. Free-flowing discussions.
- Peer counseling, learning partnerships, and online support groups.
- Simulations.

- Collective databases.
- Shared Web sites.
- Brainstorming and idea generating. This implies divergent thinking, verbalizing, and then sharing of ideas and positions, idea linking, and intellect convergence.
- Group projects. Include team meetings and collaborative online writings.
- Case studies. You could use a case study involving the telecommunications industry to discuss the pros and cons of deregulation. The online portion would expose students to basic concepts and case background. The face to face could be structured such that each student plays a particular role (e.g., industry representative, regulating agency, commission, citizen, or lobbyist) during a class session that ends when the decision-making body renders a decision.
- Debates. Instructor selects controversial topic (with input from class), then divides the class into subtopic pairs of one critic and one defender. These pairs then formulate and post positions on topic, rebut, and reply.
- Games. Games have at the heart of them a fun contest, from which emerges a winner based on skill, chance, or a combination of both. For a classroom application, the contest needs to be fun, to have set rules that create a fair playing field, and to illuminate the idea that participants emerge as winners and learners—no losers involved. Games incorporated as projects, grouped or coupled with the requirement of teamwork, not only encourage but also produce collaboration.
- Online collaborative experiments. For example, students can view patient information and diagnostic options, try out diagnosis, and see consequences of their decisions.
- Authentic data analysis.
- Role Plays. Involves creativity, training, and decision making. Students learn how to interact with different people, assume the persona of a role (students assume voice of that person for one or more sessions), enter a debate topic, or respond to a debate topic in that persona.
    - Role possibilities. Scholar, summarizer, starter, insighter, critic, devil's advocate, optimist, idea generator, coach, questioner, re-

porter, recorder, materials manager, Webmaster, technician, harmonizer, facilitator.

- Perform within roles. Try to refer to different personalities or viewpoints in peer commenting
- Email interviews.
- Critical friends. Partner with a peer to provide weekly feedback on his or her work and to give reminders and help as needed.
- Symposia or speakers on theme. Invite a panel discussion. Have them prepare statements, invite questions from the class, and assign panelists.
- Guest or expert forums. Invite a person associated with course readings, hold chat, pose questions, discuss, and debrief (ask, "Did anyone change his or her mind due to what came out of the discussion?").
- Students as experts. Have each student choose an area in which to become expert and to moderate a forum for the class. Require participation in a certain number of forums (students' choice).
- Collaborative online writing. Peer-to-peer document collaboration: planning, drafting, and reviewing of shared ideas.
- Gallery tours. Assign topic or project and students post comments.
- Field trips.
- Webquests. A strategy for scaffolding higher-level learning, it is an inquiry-based, doable, engaging task, where students use predefined sources from the Web and outside to research a topic, which can either be short or long term (Dodge, 1998).

Designing Collaborative and Constructive Web Tasks

Authentic learning provides a variety of contexts and viewpoints and helps the student see the personal and group relevance of the content. Group relevance is key because the student needs to be able to look beyond personal relevance and consider ideas from the group's point of view. Most individuals will become quickly uninterested if they cannot at least take a topic to the group level. Allow for and encourage students to share their own knowledge, opinions, and feelings about course topics and issues. Students feel heard, valued, and validated when their opinions are paraphrased by the instructor.

- Reflective/Metacognitive learning. Reflective thinking is often the ultimate goal, in journals and posts. (Instructor can probe, ask questions, refocus, set goals, and weave and synthesize comments to encourage reflective and/or critical thinking.)
- Skills for group conflict resolution. Model effective domain and/or attitudinal gestures and nurturing "soft skills" (especially faculty and VirtCamp mentors–student leaders).
- Active learning. Learner must be active in learning process. Learning is a process of construction, for example, designing projects, Web pages, animation, and video.
- Students are involved in active creation of knowledge and meaning.
- Case-based and simulated learning enacts events in roles online.
- Apprenticeship. Ask an expert, Q&A, an apprenticeship in making change while working under a mentor.
- Online resources, places, and people make possible online learning communities.
- Distribute lists of participants so students can easily contact one another.
- Cohort Web page or Web site collaboratively built and shared.
- Take courses in a program together (i.e., same time schedule).
- T-shirts and cohort name chosen by students.
- Allow students to create a shared goal for learning that is mutually negotiated.
- Have students post their assignments and encourage feedback to one another on their work, partnering to achieve learning goals

One strategy that works well is to have a student, or a team of students, teach a concept that will be covered in your course. If he or she is teaching alone, he or she should provide some informational material, comments, and examples of how the information is to be used or applied to the subject area, and then open up the discussion to the rest of the group for comments and feedback. Of course, the instructor is always the final authority, or at least someone who can straighten out confusing comments, but acting as presenter really makes students think about the application of a concept and how to get it across.

BEST PRACTICES

Best practices are those strategies, activities, or approaches to learning and teaching that have been shown through research and evaluation to be effective in the cultural environment. The term "best practice" is a subjective term because what works for one educator or institution might not work for another. We have put together a suggested list of best practices. When setting up your Web-based class you can use this checklist as a guide. Pick and choose those elements that are most appropriate for your teaching style. Integrate those that you feel will most enhance your course and the learner's experience.

Best Practices Checklist

We have included four categories of general ideas to use as a checklist in guiding your practice. When considering collaboration, activities, online protocol, and feedback/assessment, we ask that you use the following questions to form your teaching practices into best practices.

Collaboration

- Does the course design encourage and support students' social interactions?
- Do you have some content in which the students can interact so students learn from one another?
- Do you have the class divided into opportunities to work in smaller groups and engage in community-based activities?
- Do small group and large group activities complement one another?
- Do you create groups with individual accountability that support learning for all participants with interdependence so all group members must participate?
- Do you have rich and complex group projects?
- Do you do role plays, online debates, group presentations, or other stimulating variations for student interaction online?

- Do you provide guidance on teamwork and encourage collaboration rather than competition?

Activities

- Do you have audio and video lectures online that go beyond "talking heads" to explain and demonstrate course expectations?
- Do you have fit-for-purpose online activities?
- Do you have synchronized powerpoint slideshows that compliment your lectures online?
- Do you utilize WebQuests, virtual tours, or other online resource activities?
- Do you have any interactive simulations and multimedia?
- Do you incorporate guest speakers or outside content experts into course activities?
- Have you turned some of your quizzes into games?

Online Protocol

- Do you provide etiquette and common rules for Web interactions?
- Do you encourage or mandate that students help one another, answer one another's questions online, or otherwise assist and engage in sharing in the group?

Feedback/Assessment

- Do you have multiple ways of evaluation and grading?
- Do you have assessments for group activities?
- Do you offer corrective feedback with detailed notes and a grade?
- Do you have unit self quizzes in which the student can gain feedback but are not a part of the student's grade?
- Do you provide midpoint grade notification for students who need to improve?
- Do you save student testimonials about your course to share with future students?
- Do you provide exemplary examples of desired writing and assignments?

TRANSLATING INSTRUCTOR PRESENCE ONLINE

Instructors have to hold the community that they establish together and have effective communication skills in order for the class to succeed. To achieve this goal, instructors need to make themselves readily available not only in the academic arena but also in the personal sense by establishing relationships with their students that show they are available and ready to work with each student individually and as a group. Learning is a social endeavor and as such needs social context, which includes the instructor/facilitator.

In a regular educational setting, where the instructor and students meet face-to-face in a classroom or environment of their choosing, it is very easy for there to be relationships built through the usual methods of communication—talking, eye contact, body language, and personal and group conversations. Students quickly gain an idea of how their instructor will interact with them (Will there be joking around? Is this instructor serious and to the point?) and what kind of relationships will form in the classroom. However, when teaching an online class all the normal cues a person would use to read another person are absent. In most cases, text is the method of communication. In the online arena, educators now have the added task of translating their personalities online so that the students can develop a relationship with them and see them as the caring and nurturing people that they are in real life. It is important for instructors to keep in mind that it is up to them to develop the atmosphere that will enhance each student's learning. They will have to put themselves out there, on the line, and hope that their personalities shine through. As one student commented to another about my online presence during the teaching of a course: "I agree with your perception of Mercedes, Arthur. I was in one of the early TI sessions in which I felt I was truly a student learning in TI—(synchronous sessions) instead of just talking. Asking questions of my prof., receiving answers, but also listening to questions of others and answers of the group. I noticed that she encouraged us to listen to her conversations with each of us and I appreciated that. Even though this slowed the pace some, I felt it was more valuable" (Neena, September 9, 2002). It is important to model the behavior you wish your students to exhibit by interacting with them in the most meaningful way possible in order to facilitate their learning.

The instructor's daily presence in the course discussions is crucial. The instructor needs to be actively involved every weekday in the threaded discussion for that week—responding to students' comments, initiating follow-up questions, making sure the discussion stays interesting and alive. In our experience, teachers who have a clear presence in their course discussion, those who add to the discussion as participants more than as authoritative instructors, generate better cohort dialogue patterns.

Pose provocative online discussion questions that require students to know the facts and key concepts yet also to think critically about the subject matter. Instructors should illustrate this by sharing their experiences in these particular areas. The discussions are usually the students' favorite part of the course, so developing good discussion questions goes a long way toward giving students the intrinsic desire to stay in the class, rather than the extrinsic motivator of discipline, pleasing the instructor, or even grades, to some extent.

Students can help one another out a lot in some ways, but there is no substitute for an instructor's close reading of students' work—or for his or her very detailed feedback. Frequent feedback is needed from the instructor. Feedback needs to be given in discussion and assessment. You are seen as a mentor and your direction is welcomed. Remember that narrative feedback is more helpful and will quickly be a motivator to students; eventually it will be more of a motivator than the grade. When there is a graded activity, it is essential that feedback and the grade are given in a timely manner. Teacher decisions and direct involvement needs to be visible so that students can see the teacher is processing what they are saying. If the design for assessment is clear, the learner will be able to target a deeper understanding for information rather than just scratching at surface knowledge that might not lead them to see the big idea of the topic at hand.

Be a Facilitator, Not a Controller

Facilitation is an important aspect of the online learning community. The instructor must act as the facilitator in the discussion without controlling the discussion. Preferably, facilitators should coordinate discussions and encourage participation, but at the same time, they should avoid being identified with authority. This implies discussions in which self-directed as well as peer-to-peer collaborative learning is supported, in which the teacher–expert acts as a "guide on the side" rather than as a "sage on the stage" (Guzdial and Weingarten, 1995). Learners will take a topic of discussion, usually presented by the facilitator, in a direction that they need to discuss most. Avoid being the expert/mentor every time a student makes a comment. Instead, be quiet, allowing others the chance to respond, giving alternative points of view. Help students analyze the ideas tactfully, and redirect students who dominate the discussion.

One of the issues for us has been recognizing the value of spending time with depth (i.e., staying with the process and the group's concerns, including identifying and confronting the issues) rather than breadth (i.e., more and more content—the old teaching expert paradigm). Perceptive learning moments may be squelched if the instructor cannot keep out of the discussion once it gets going. The instructor may also assign a student to be the facilitator, in which case the instructor then simply monitors the progress, offers support, and herds the class. Like Poole, we found participation in the course changed when students served as course moderators, suggesting the positive effect such a role may have on learning and community building. Whether the facilitator is the instructor or an assigned student, there are typical functions for this role that have proven to be the most successful, which include developing objectives, assembling and managing teams or groups, determining and managing student expectations, monitoring topic schedules and the time allotted for breakout, and identifying and resolving problems. The nature of the discussions as being more direct, interactive, and flexible has brought about a renewed interest in classroom social interaction.

The preference is to be with the students as a peer in the journey, even though you have been engaged to lead them. You have been partway yourself, so you can show them that part and point out some of the pitfalls, but even this is likely to take you where you haven't been yet. Students experience empowerment (Engelbart, 1995; Norman, 1993), allowing learners to incrementally acquire ownership in and to actively contribute to the resolution of challenges (Arias, 1999). As participants act upon a problem, breakdowns occur due to incomplete understanding of the underlying problem, conflicts among perspectives, or the absence of shared understanding. By supporting the process of reflection within these discussions that provide a shared context, opportunities arise for building upon these breakdowns in ways that integrate the various perspectives and expertise while enhancing shared understanding. Supporting informed participation requires processes that integrate the individual and the group knowledge through collaborative constructions (Arias, 1999). Without acknowledging needs such as empowerment, freedom, fun, and belonging, we will not be successful in addressing the challenges faced by authentic real-world learning situations. An effective instructor should:

- Be mentally prepared and provide constructive coaching and feedback.
- Be accurate.
- Clarify misunderstandings and be available to resolve differences.
- Refer to comments and resources made by other students.
- Summarize or center discussions when off track.
- Raise questions.

Model Behavior and Expectations

It is important for instructors to model the behavior and quality of work that they expect from their students in the way they act themselves. Showing the students by example how to use the threaded discussions, newsgroups, converse in a chat session, perform research, or pose a question will help those students unsure of format to participate. Model and expect professional-level communications from your students when they are engaged in professional discussions. This includes using correct capital letters, punctuation, grammar, syntax, and spelling to the best of their ability, as well as staying focused on the etiquette of a discussion. Communication standards are key and should you, as the instructor, request responses at a certain time, try to hold yourself to the same time frame. Setting a response time will allow you to see those students who have been keeping up or pinpoint those who may be slipping behind. If you set a clear course agenda, students will be able to focus on the objectives and be able to follow the timetable progression successfully through the course. You should attempt to provide enough structure for the learners to feel comfortable but allow for flexibility and negotiation of course content. Having such an open-door policy allows all involved to be comfortable to change procedures that are not working for the group. Some guidelines and procedures for collaboration among students in groups can be loose and free flowing.

Guidelines and Instructions

Guidelines are especially useful when teaching an online class because of a lack of the usual cues students and teachers would use to understand one another. As in the guidelines discussed earlier for online chat sessions, other guidelines such as "norms," a set of rules of conduct, for threaded discussions are useful, and can be developed along with the students at the beginning of the course so that everyone knows how to act. They can be as simple or as complicated as the students. Norms can also be developed throughout the journey of the course as situations occur. Interactions help determine community norms.

Instructions should be given clearly and concisely. Make sure that you allow students time to ask questions as needed. Listen to comments and concerns and address them as necessary, whether via email, threaded discussions, or in a synchronous group discussion. The class projects, discussions, products, and presentations are clear outcomes for knowledge. Rubrics are made to establish standards so students have knowledge of the expectations. The rubrics set parameters for student endeavors. Projects have the potential to clarify the purpose of learning for students. Measuring depth of understanding can pose challenges for objectivity. Clear, concise, and detailed rubrics can help with this interpretation and provide effective communication. There are thousands of Web sites that provide teachers with pre-made rubrics in any number of subject areas. Ultimately, the most useful rubrics are those you create yourself. Frequently, I have my students describe models and rubrics, and we build them together so they are invested in the process, and in my experience they work hard to live up to expectations they have helped define.

Narrative Feedback

Students depend on constructive feedback in order for their abilities to progress and advance. Be sure to give details and add helpful and insightful comments where appropriate. Encourage learners to make active use of feedback to improve their final output/product. Encourage students to ask for feedback during the course if they feel they have not received enough from you. At the same time, it is good for you to allow students to provide you with feedback on your abilities as an instructor and if you are meeting their needs.

Humor

It is always important to remember that many situations can easily be defused with a little humor. Everyone appreciates attempts to create a lighthearted atmosphere where people feel comfortable enough to laugh and to interact with one another. As the instructor, you should be aware of the climate within your group and try to encourage jokes here and there. If you are going to make jokes, do it before you need humor to defuse a tense situation, and if a class member is a natural comedian, make sure you laugh early and often so they feel comfortable "LOL-ing" (laughing out loud) too.

Props

This can include anything from cartoons, news clippings, articles, photos, pictures, analogies, and animations—anything that can help you teach in a more effective and enjoyable manner. Use these props to create discussion with students, relating them to their outside lives and encouraging them to bring their experiences and stories to the class in the hope of creating a more meaningful learning environment for all.

Profiles

Students appreciate information about their professors and instructors. It helps them feel as though they know you personally if you have a little background about yourself—biographical info, academic/business experience, personal background (family, hobbies, etc.), digital photographs, picture-portrait layouts—on your Web site or your school's Web site. Figures 4.7 and 4.8 are examples from my course Web site of my personal and professional information.

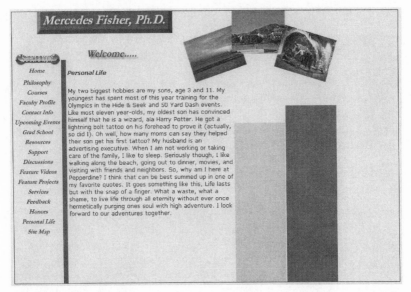

Figure 4.7. *Personal Life*

Effective Techniques to Consider

Below is a summary list of the most effective techniques an instructor can use in building community, maintaining communication, and achieving an overall successful online course:

Administrative

- Provide timely information about syllabi, books, enrollment, and counseling.
- Outline conceptual knowledge to be covered in the syllabus, principles of best practice, and guidelines for application in work settings.
- Create the syllabus as a "skin," which is thematically organized and contains print, video, and Web references, as well as assignments.
- Keep in mind the primary goals with this style—critical thinking, developing student interests, collaboration, and discussion.
- Deal promptly with inappropriate behavior, whining, dominance, and harassment. The sun never sets on the online course, so handle problems in a timely fashion.

< Back to the Faculty Index

Mercedes Fisher, Ph.D.
Associate Professor of Education

B.A., Austin College; M.A., Austin College; Ph.D., University of Denver. Pepperdine University since 2000.

Dr. Fisher has knowledge of and experience with urban K-12 schools, curriculum development, designing collaborative learning models online, learning theory, instructional design, technology management, and e-learning. She has published research articles in international journals and presented her research as an invited speaker at various international meetings and conferences. Dr. Fisher was named Fulbright Senior Specialist Scholar in March 2002. Prior to Pepperdine, she was a three time Distinguished Scholar at Marquette University. She takes pride in her teaching and brings her own special curiosity, genuine positive attitude, compassion and successful experiences to the classroom. Recently, she has worked with grants from Microsoft Corporation, the U.S. Department of Education, Technology Literacy Challenge, and Wisconsin Department of Public Instruction. In 1997, she was selected as an International Group Study Exchange Team Member to study the development of online teaching and learning resources in Denmark and Germany. Prior to Marquette, she taught at the University of Southern Colorado and received both the Outstanding Faculty Award and the Faculty Advisor of the Year for the 1995-1996 school year. She also served as the Director of the Beck-Ortner Technology Center, and conducted research emphasizing instructional design and technology applied to classroom learning. Prior to USC, she taught middle school and high school in Texas and Colorado. Dr. Fisher co-directs the Master of Arts program in educational technology, a WASC-approved online program in Educational Technology, which enrolls students from across the globe.

Contact: mmfisher@pepperdine.edu

Figure 4.8.   *Faculty and Staff Page*

- Design quick intervention for non-participators, especially if it becomes a group issue.

Plan

- Resist the urge to overload activities. Keep in mind that communication usually takes longer in an online class. Give students time to interact and assimilate the information.

- Connect students and course content to literature that is meaning-ful to them.
- Present crucial content in multiple media formats.
- Set up a well-organized course site that includes resources, books (figure 4.9), learner-centered syllabus, best student work (figure 4.10), contact information, and support resources (figure 4.11). Consider setting up a mentors gallery for virtual faculty develop-ment, too, if time and resources are available.
- Involve outside experts on topics related to training and for idea generation on products.

Build Community

- Demonstrate instructor approachability through humor and open-ness.
- Be sensitive to language, momentum, and mood of class.
- Be able to recognize a "teachable moment" during a discussion, and expand the conversation in that moment.
- Coach students through practice.
- Be flexible, patient, and responsive; maintain a non-authoritarian style.
- Avoid lecturing (long, coherent sequences of comments by the in-structor yields silence). The point here is let the books, assigned articles, and position papers do the lecturing if needed. The differ-ence in reading speed precludes effective long windedness during Internet classes.
- Avoid directives, leading students to your point of view, and "right" answers. Let students discover their own path.

Design

- Use multiple teaching and learning strategies to engage students in active learning opportunities that promote the development of crit-ical thinking, problem solving, and performance capabilities. Choose strategies that help students to reach their proficiency re-sponsibility, using computer program(s) as a learning tool.
- Integrate the backward-design process to promote the use of a multifaceted, project-based curriculum design.

Mentoring
and Team Leadership

EDC 639 - Mentoring and Team Leadership

Introduction
This course should support work you are doing in your ARP and elsewhere this trimester. Let me know if it isn't. There are two foci for the course: a "long view" and an immediate view. The focus is on you. How can you be a successful mentor and educational leader? The overarching question for the trimester is the consideration of the relationship between teaching, learning, and mentoring. This should relate directly back to your readings in EDC 633.

The descriptions of mentoring represented in the literature-to-date have evolved from a view of learning that is derived from a behavioral or cognitive psychology of the individual, a notion that knowledge resides in the head and is acquired (cognitive), or that it is a matter of habit strength attained by reinforced practice (behavioral). As you know from ED. 633, there are newer views of learning as a social experience, as enculturation if you will. And views of knowledge as distributed among community members and embedded in practice. There are no mentoring texts, yet, written from a CoP or sociocultural historical psychology perspective. We'll have to figure out the implications of that theory for our actions as mentors and team leaders in our work settings.

I also hope to engage you in some sustained deep constructive uses of computers in order to reinforce your understanding of constructivism.

Course Overview
We're going to try a variety of "mentoring and team leadership" activities. First, you are going to enter into a mentoring relationship with one or two individuals. You will also work collaboratively on two projects concerned with critical issues facing contemporary educators and preparing educators for learning and teaching in the future.

During our first face-to-face class, I will assign folks to a quartet of fellow students. A quartet will provide intellectual and moral support for members. Office hours will be conducted with quartets.

You will be asked to keep a running log of your efforts. That log will be highly structured by me (see below).

Our online sessions will have three goals:
1) to discuss what we have read and think about what it means for what we are doing;
2) to discuss what you are doing in your coursework and identify critical issues;
3) to consider the differences between individual and larger group efforts.

Figure 4.9. *Mentoring and Team Leadership*

Student Project Examples

Action Research
Staff Development
Curriculum Design
Active Learning
Classroom Community of Practice
Museum Development

Distributed Learning Environments
Lab/Virt Camp
Lego Challenge-Hard Fun
Movie
Project Description Page

Interactive Projects (EDC 640)
plugin for Microworlds or Flash required
Treasure Island
Sonia's Pet
Dawg
Terry Tadpole
Quetzalbee
Achieving Albert
Goldfish
Ice Fishing
Teenage Samantha
The Boxer
Gophers
Thunderhead
Mini-Doug

Curriculum and Technology
Corporate and Educational Training
Workshop (Distance Learning)
Coaching Workshop
Creativity Workshop
Multimedia Workshop
Lesson Design Workshop
Curriculum Workshop

Education
Curriculum Brainstorm
Research Article Review (pdf)
Curriculum Brainstorm/Workshop Idea
Curriculum Brainstorm
Curriculum Idea
Language Arts Curriculum
Software Evaluation

Case Studies (Technology)
High School
Knowledge Sharing
Sociology
Language Arts
Elementary School
High School

Learning and Technology (EDC 664)
Example Blueprint
Learning Blueprint
Example Projects
Early Childhood and Beyond
QTVR
Wireless Website Creation
iMovie
Web Graphics and Design
Historical Recreation
Fundamentals of Flying
Direct Deposit Option

Managing Technology
Radio Streaming
Open Mike

Community of Practice
Workplace Example

Other good projects
Web Design

Figure 4.10.   *Feature Projects*

- Develop a group learning experience where participants work to-gether via the Internet/Web as a cohort in completing program courses.
- Create highly interactive online learning activities that stimulate analysis through discussion. Facilitate a discussion by providing examples of "how to" interact (e.g., conflict resolution, following

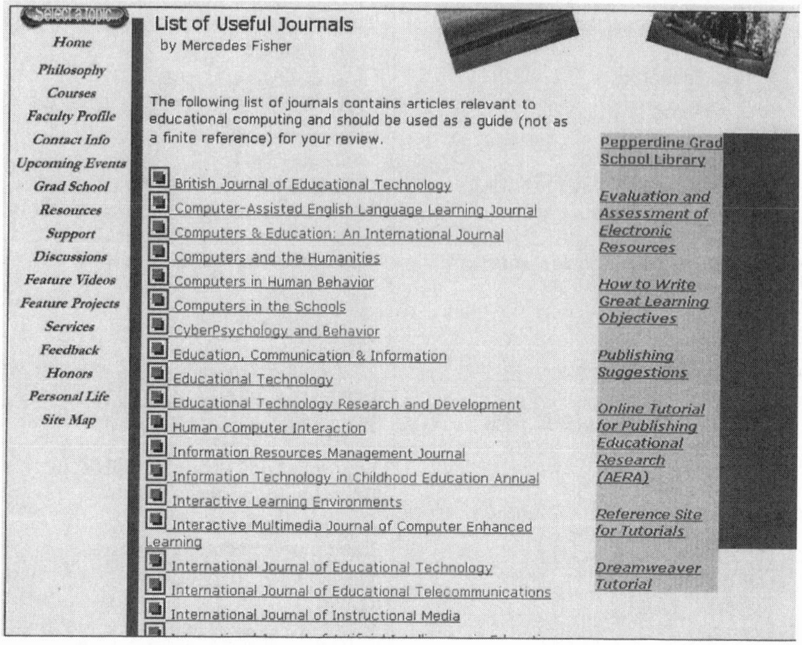

Figure 4.11. *Student Resources*

a topic in depth, and not having too many conversations at one time as it dilutes the focus).

- Maintain flexibility to incorporate time-sensitive data as well as links to freshly mounted Web sites; add new links and breaking news on topics.
- Design opportunities for students to work through problems, experiments, or scenario-based simulations presented online and to compare their solutions.

Discussion

- Provide a variety of interesting and relevant discussion topics and resources.
- Facilitate activities that engage the learner. As the students progress, you can help them focus by modeling questioning skills; listening; providing effective feedback, direction, and support; managing discussion; motivating; building relation-

ships and teams; taking risks; and highlighting relevance to workplace.

- Monitor and react to individual student participation.
- Sense the overall direction of the class.
- Be responsive to the group. Instructor reads and summarizes responses before real-time class discussion (chat) and weaves them into the discussion and changes the focus/presentation/lecture as appropriate; new and different ideas become clarified, identified, and clustered into various positions.
- Acknowledge contributions.
- Support others for e-moderator role.
- Promote continuity within the communication.
- Wrap up or close unproductive discussions or conversations promptly.

Model

- Model and encourage students to bring real-life examples into the online classroom. The more relevant the material is to their lives, the more likely they are to integrate it into the learning experience.
- Model online interactivity.
- Publish examples of best practice (student work).

CONTINUOUS IMPROVEMENT

The Internet is changing how we interact with knowledge. Technology facilitates learning at a different level, and when used as a learning tool it can greatly enhance the learning experience. For continuous improvement, we need to focus on new and innovative processes, Web tools being one of them. Learning is in a transformative stage today. Students need to be problem solvers, creative thinkers, and self-directed learners to be successful in their chosen careers. Our challenge is to create learning environments that facilitate and develop these skills.

Design processes are being transformed to be more adaptive, generative, and scalable. Computer-aided design allows for customization by modifying variables and parameters and adjusting shareable content objects, templates, and interface platforms. The range of new information-technology tools and resources continues to become faster, cheaper, and more useful and allows for an unprecedented degree of connectedness of knowledge, experience, media, and people.

Cognitive skills are being implemented more effectively on the Web with data, facts, and figures. Previous face-to-face, in-person learning turns into detailed and frequent discussions on the Web. Students can access all or parts of the Web-based course at their optimal learning time and place (e.g., late at night or after 10 A.M., when students are most receptive to learning and can max out their attention and focus). Students can learn parts of courses at their own speed. The Web-based course allows students the opportunity to go over the content material as many times as needed. Often, students go over the content material with increasing levels of understanding and participation. One can go back and review emails or transcripts from online discussions. I really like this perspective. I try to use many and varied media in courses where the students, building a common frame of reference, share their experience.

Doing this course as a learning experience and then commenting interpersonally on it allows the individual to relate his- or herself reflectively to the shared experience. Most of the time, more participants are actively involved in online discussions than in a face-to-face discussion because there are more resources to learn online. "Doing this course as in experiencing the doing" is what's exciting —and leads to an individualized expression of a shared experience. The experience of "doing" the course is as valuable as the material that is done. The shared "doing" of the course creates a level of understanding that is deep, beautiful, and varied like a kaleidoscope. Resources that can be utilized by the group include the use of video, audio, lectures, and visuals. Authorities and experts on topics can be brought in to speak, and the session can be broadcasted to the whole group at once.

The virtual community usually enables the learning to be extended beyond the course as the participants move on and continue to learn and pull in information from the many resources available. Much more of a personal learning shift takes place in the online learning environment. Movement away from information transfer and direct instruction is common. Some examples from Web sites are read in chunks, clicking on links, digging deeper, seldom scrolling down. It is not a linear process of transfer but more of a fluid and shared process. We can scan and discover learning activities that are student centered in the Web-based learning environment. Software is needed to view motion and sound from video, audio, multimedia, and animation (examples of software tutorials are in appendix C). Much online material can be presented using media players that show the student how to do something step by step. The evaluation could require the student to complete a task and be provided with instant feedback for each step accomplished correctly or incorrectly.

The instructor is the designer; this lets you build a course that is very personalized and has mass customization of content. I have found that students learn better when the professor effectively utilizes scaffolding, gives students choices, uses frameworks for analysis and support, models critical reflection, and uses a variety of instructional approaches. Some of the methods I have adopted include cooperative learning, simulations, instructional and tool software, field experiences, demonstrations, guest speakers, videos of real teaching situations, "hands on" projects, and class discussion. Connecting field-based experiences to my courses has provided students with opportunities to reflect on practical experiences, to interpret and apply the theories they are studying, and to relate them in ways that help them articulate and refine their perspectives on concepts, the workplace, and their own values.

Many courses are offered solely on the Web, and many more are Web enhanced by blending learning using face-to-face and Web tools. We see the need for team building even in individual courses. Most online teaching situations don't have this advantage. We need to make sure to address the community building ideas from the perspective of a single-semester course with a group of students that has probably never worked together before and probably won't be together in another course. Online learning takes place in the classroom, not just at a distance. Education is becoming an activity not a place. Albert Einstein wrote, "Learning is experience; everything else is information." We are not isolated with a machine; rather we have extended human capabilities and the potential to network because of our use with the computer and Internet.

CHAPTER 5

Evaluating the Student
Mercedes Fisher with Peita Ramos

To begin with the end in mind means to start with a clear understanding of your destination. It means to know where you are going so that you better understand where you are not so that the steps you take are always in the right direction.

—Stephen R. Covey, *The Seven Habits of Highly Effective People*

The notion that learning comes about by the accretion of little bits is outmoded learning theory. Current models of learning based on cognitive psychology contend that learners gain understanding when they construct their own knowledge and develop their own cognitive maps of the interconnections among facts and concepts . . . . Real learning cannot be spoon-fed one skill at a time.

— Lori Shepard, Assessing Students' Performance

CREATING AND OPTIMIZING ASSESSMENT STRATEGIES

Assessments should be developed based on student contributions, in conjunction with the pre-planned course material. It is important as part of your planning that you establish first what you want students to know and be able to do by the end of the course, setting standards that accompany these goals. When designing curriculum units, Wiggins and McTighe, two leaders in the revolution of standards and assessment design, advocate using a "backwards design" method (1998). When using this method, you start with the goals and standards you have for your particular course and then work backward, designing the curriculum and learning activities for your students from the performance task (the evidence of proficiency for the standard) that will best prepare your students to do well. Using this backward-design method, or backward mapping (Spady, 1994b), helps learners keep a clear picture in their mind of what the goals and big ideas for the course will be and helps construct their learning into what can be referred to as "enduring understanding." It is also important to keep in mind the following guiding questions when designing curriculum:

1. What action can be taken to create an environment of enduring understanding?
2. What is important to be able to know and do?
3. What is worth being familiar with?

All effective assessment must be connected to clear learning outcomes that tie in with your course standards, goals, and big ideas. Ideally, personalized and meaningful outcomes for learners are consistent with the outcomes defined in your curriculum. Learning outcomes should be created with precise verbs used to specify the expected level of thinking and performance. When specifying these criteria for evaluating learning and performance, use three or four levels to assist students in choosing what grade they want to strive for. This will also allow students to self-assess as they work through their learning.

Although you do not want the focus to be on letter grades, students need to know what your expectations are for student participation and quality of assignments. Write out clear directions for the performance assessment by using incremental deadlines. It is key for assessments to be tied to discussion-participation grades in your rubrics and to note that you will be expecting peer evaluation for participation in small-group assignments. In addition to a clear rubric, it is important to provide regular qualitative and quantitative feedback, preferably in a narrative style. Irrespective of how well students are performing in our courses, we found them to be subsequently less successful at the tasks, and reported less interest in those tasks, if they received a grade rather than narrative feedback. Other research (Kohn, 2002) has produced the same result: Grades almost always have a detrimental effect on how well students learn and how interested they are in the topic they're learning. From this, it is important to consider adding some narrative feedback to your Web courses.

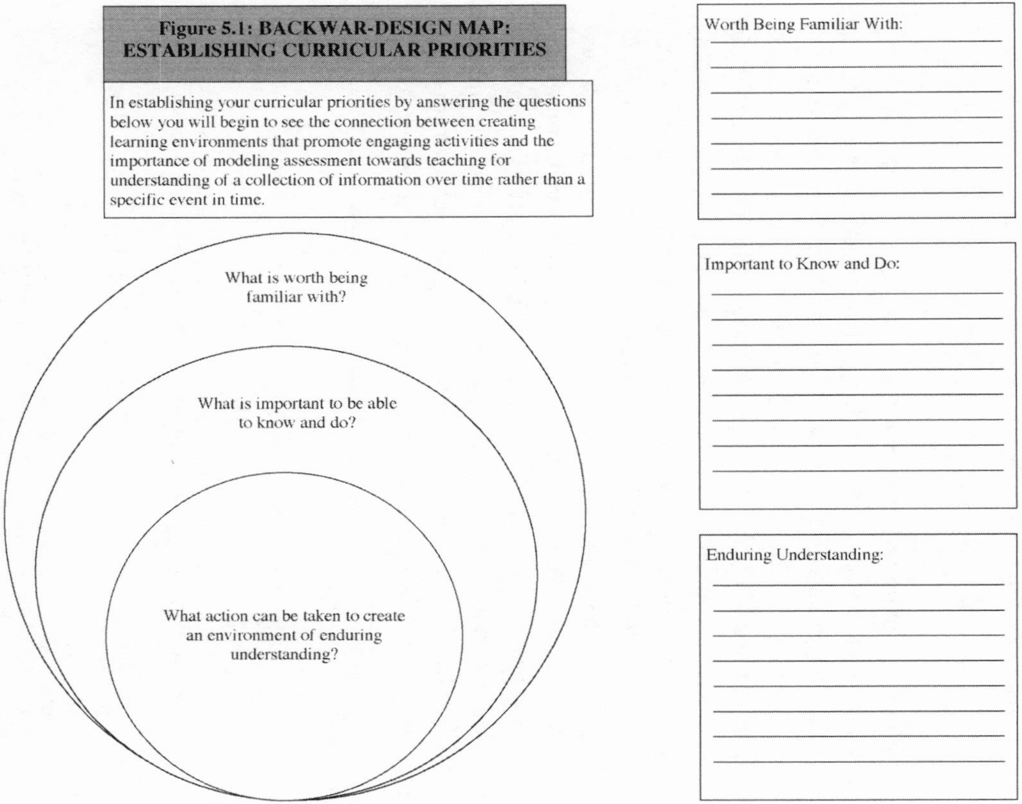
Figure 5.1: BACKWAR-DESIGN MAP:
ESTABLISHING CURRICULAR PRIORITIES
In establishing your curricular priorities by answering the questions below you will begin to see the connection between creating learning environments that promote engaging activities and the importance of modeling assessment towards teaching for understanding of a collection of information over time rather than a specific event in time.
What is worth being familiar with?
What is important to be able to know and do?
What action can be taken to create an environment of enduring understanding?
Worth Being Familiar With:
Important to Know and Do:
Enduring Understanding:

Figure 5.1. ***Backward-Design Map***

HOW TO MEASURE STUDENT LEARNING

> Carefully crafted assessments would ask students to supply an-
> swers, perform observable acts, demonstrate skills, create products,
> and supply portfolios of work.
>
> —National Commission on Testing and Public Policy, 1991

It is important that throughout your course, students demonstrate proficiency at essential skills and knowledge that you have determined as
goals at the beginning of the course. There needs to be a wide range of
methods employed with your students to assess their learning. Learning in the real world does not take place using a multiple-choice test, in
the same way, learning for understanding cannot be assessed using only
one type of traditional-style assessment such as tests and quizzes. Assessment needs to be based on real-world examples that are authentic,
challenging, diverse, and enjoyable. This will allow students to use
complex reasoning and communication skills, placing value on the assessment in such a way that it is meaningful and powerful for your students. Tasks should be scaffolded in such a way that learning and understanding builds one on top of the other, taking the learner from being
a novice to showing exemplary work. Figure 5.2 is an example of a

---

Tips for this assignment:

- Should be done at the midpoint of the semester and again, at the end of the
  semester.

- Two documents, submitted in the same format. Doc #1 would cover the first
  half of the term and Doc #2 would cover the second half of the term.

- Posted in threaded discussion or emailed privately to the professor (this is up
  to the instructor).

- Each document would cover 2-3 postings the student made, which they feel
  moved the class forward by contributing to understanding, and 2-3 postings
  others made that contributed to their deeper understanding.

- In the student's response (post) to this assignment request that they embed
  the whole posting, headers and all, as it will help the instructor to situate the
  posting. Encourage the student to think about other ways of supporting that
  context and to include information in the threaded discussion summary on
  other people's posts that impacted them.

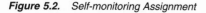

Figure 5.2.   *Self-monitoring Assignment*

self-monitoring assignment that allows learners to document over time their collaboration in threaded discussions. The assignment was originally suggested to us by previous students as a way for them to self-monitor their own quality of participation in the asynchronous part of the course. It provides a quality indicator that is distinct from quantity.

We recommend that when designing a curriculum unit, you choose to use both formative and summative assessments to achieve the best results for your students and the most accurate view of their learning.

TYPES OF ASSESSMENTS

When designing your assessment items, you should keep in mind the many learning styles of your students. It is important that you don't continually use one type of assessment item, as it might not work for the majority. Even if it does work for a majority, you should still mix up assessment types so that all of the students have an opportunity to be assessed in a wide range of tasks. After all, you want your students to be able to do the best they can, and creating differed and varying assignments will keep your students interested and engaged in the course content. We believe it's not about students simply doing the best they can; multiple, varied assessment provides multiple perspectives on understanding. This type of narrative feedback over a wide variety of performances extends the learning environment so that learning continues to take place during both evaluation and reflection phases.

Before you start teaching, you might want to administer a pre-course-needs assessment or background survey such as a KWL pre-test (see section in chapter 2, "Creating a Web Site for Your Course"). Assessments such as these will identify the needs of your students as they come into your course as well as their current level of background knowledge with the course content. Figure 5.3 shows us an example of a pre-assessment survey that allows you to gather a great deal of information in an informal way. By showing that you are aware of their needs and issues, it shows that you are willing to work with them and will enhance the students' openness to the course content you are presenting. It will help in creating an atmosphere of learning together and break down the barriers between teacher and students, leading to a cohesive community environment.

I have listed seven top features of Microsoft Word 2002. Descriptions of features are listed as the uses for each. Please rank these features from 1 to 7 (1 being your first choice). The top four features will be selected.

Feature	Description of Feature	What would I use that for?	Rank (1-7)
Compare and Merge Feature	This feature allows for collaboration in the development of reports. Multiple personnel can review a document and combine them in one document.	• If you collaborate on group reports, you can combine everyone's comments and then decide which comments to keep and which to discard.	
Mail Merge	This feature allows you create one main document and join with a listing of names and addresses to produce multiple letters.	• Create form letters without the hassle of doing them individually. • Create mailing labels from a list of names, addresses you have on your computer. • Create phone lists from existing lists in Excel, Word, Access or Filemaker.	
Online Forms	This feature allows you to create forms. You can send these forms out to be completed. This feature allows you to lock your form so you will receive them in the same format you sent with information.	• Do you frequently have to create forms? • Do your forms come back misaligned and nothing like you sent them. • Generate surveys for students, staff and faculty.	
Reviewers Comments	This feature allows you to enter electronic comments to document.	• Reviews other's reports and insert your comments and email. • Grade online student work with comments.	
Styles/ Templates	Styles allow you to save formatting effects (font, color, alignment, size) and apply them quickly to other areas in a document.	• Do you have reports that require certain font sizes, fonts, alignments? This will speed up your work. • Do you frequently have to alter the visual effects on the document? This will make it a snap.	
Tables	Tables allow you to display textual, graphical or numeric information for reports, emails or presentations. Setting up a table, inserting and deleting rows/columns will be covered. Quick formatting will be reviewed.	• If you have lots of numeric information in a report or email and want to balance on a page, this is for you. • If you have frequent rush jobs and don't have time to "make it pretty", the quick formatting techniques will make you job look better.	
Tabs/ Alignment	The tabs and alignment features in Word are important for making documents look professional. What are they and how to se	• Are you tired of hitting the tab button over and over again to get stuff to line up? • Would you like to know how to make your paragraphs even on each side?	

Created by V. Karnes 2003

Figure 5.3. Sample Pre-assessment Survey

Throughout both the units and the course, we recommend using a variety of formative assessment techniques such as unit-module quizzes, journal entries, projects, and small-group activities such as optional book groups, all of which give quick feedback along the way for participants. End-of-course projects or exams can be used as summative assessment, such as one-on-one exams or public demonstrations. Build in opportunities for reflection and self-assessment throughout the course, as this will encourage your students to look critically at their own learning and participation. We encourage the use of both individual and group work assignments when you are assessing your students because the different types of feedback provided in each of these assessment pieces differ. Remember that evaluation should focus on concepts and knowledge that are most important in the course and should be taken from the kinds of knowledge and concepts students were exposed to in the course.

Formative Assessment

Formative assessment can be one of the most powerful types of assessment for increasing student performance. It should be found throughout the course and should be placed at significant checkpoints along the way to provide the students with appropriate feedback that allows them to gain a larger understanding of their own progress. Assessment should not be limited to being given at the end of a unit but should be ongoing, allowing the students to demonstrate their learning and become effective at communicating what they have learned. Learning is an ongoing process, and students need to be able to monitor their own progress as they pass specific benchmarks. These types of assessments can be anything from classroom discussions, student-discussion groups, teacher–student observations, small tests or quizzes, student writing assignments, portfolios, and homework. Using these types of assessments allows not only the student to monitor their progress but also gives the teacher an indication of how the course is going and will enable him or her to make changes in instruction strategy or techniques throughout the course to better meet the students needs.

The use of tests and quizzes throughout the course will allow the students to monitor their progress. This is extremely important because it lets you, as the instructor, provide good narrative feedback to your stu-

dents, which shows them that you are aware of their progress or lack of
it. Not only will this enable you to monitor how effective your teaching is, to see how the assignments and activities you have planned and
are incorporating into your unit are working, but also to provide you
with information and knowledge indicating that you may need to
change or improve an assignment in order to meet your students' needs
more effectively. As the instructor, you can collect the data from these
formative assignments and act on the issues that present themselves by
forming ideas that will help students as they proceed through your
course. We do not use the formative evaluations as part of the grade.

The use of a portfolio as an assessment piece allows you to monitor
your students' progress and observe their continual improvement as
they move through the concepts of your course. By scaffolding ideas
and concepts one on top of the other, you allow the students to develop
their thinking along clear and concise paths. The types of assignments
used in the portfolio enable the students to write and communicate
about their learning using originality and depth in ways different than
tests or quizzes. Portfolios tend to be more authentic in their assessment
design, allowing students to show their understanding of a concept using methods such as written and graphical representations and share
their ideas with their own community of practice.

We would like to add to the discussion the notion of assessing the
community of learners or community of practice that your students create among themselves as a separate entity. Have your students do
assignments as a whole group, identifying the roles of a successful
community of practice among themselves and working together as
a community of shared practice toward a common end. It is important
to identify how your group is coming together and working together.
Since knowledge is shared, how do we measure the health of that community? There are several resources on the Web, such as www
.iastate.edu/~learncommunity/guidelines.html that will be useful in
helping identify best practices for community assessment.

Summative Assessment

Summative assessment is used at the end of a unit to assess students'
overall learning of the content and concepts presented in the course.

This kind of assessment looks at the learners' understanding of the concepts and usually consists of an overarching assignment that encompasses the sum of all the concepts presented in the course. Instructors need to identify how much weight a summative assessment should play in a student's final grade. They also face the dilemma of what format the summative assessment should take: Should it be only the concepts learned in the course, or should it allow the students to go beyond what was taught and apply their critical thinking and complex reasoning skills to the assignment? The most typical type of summative assessment is that of the final test or exam, which asks questions of the student to assess their real learning from the course content.

Informal Assessment

Throughout the term, poll students for formative feedback and survey student opinions. Informal assessment could take the form of anonymous online surveys of students or a virtual suggestion box. The instructor should decide how to respond to the comments given. Provide response to the comments and most or all of the suggestions in an online forum. This will defuse difficult issues, air instructor views, and justify actions publicly. Submissions could be password protected to a class or located in a class Web space. Or, you could use push technology (which "pushes" your students to respond) and email students these types of questions:

Please respond to the following questions over the next week when time permits:

1. What did you contribute to this first small-group project?
2. What do you think you personally could have done to improve this activity? What do you think you did well?
3. Did each member of your group participate? What concerns, if any, did you have about how the group worked together to complete the project? What do you think the group did particularly well in working together to complete this project?
4. Did the group demonstrate what they learned via a Web site or threaded discussion summary with a rationale for its choice?

Thanks in advance for your consideration.

Be sure to email this to me individually, rather than to the group, so that your comments will be private.

Students might also be polled with a Web form online. The instructor sends out the URL; students click on form and submit. They rank themselves and their peers (using "never," "sometimes," and "always") on categories that you believe best reflect each group member's participation (items can include the following: met deadlines for group meetings and project, shared course group environment materials and resources, active role in process, accepts responsibilities/tasks work behavior roles, communication and sharing ideas, respects different points of view, uses effective strategy, monitor and demonstrate group processes, encourages other members, documented resources, among others).

DESIGNING PERFORMANCE ASSESSMENTS

When designing an online course, one of the most important aspects to consider is the assessment pieces that you will be using to monitor the students' learning throughout the course. Performance assessments offer the students a variety of tasks and opportunities in which to demonstrate that they understand the concepts being explored. It also allows them to apply the knowledge and skills developed in a variety of different contexts. Meaningful assessment means that the students are not just required to regurgitate information on a multiple-choice test that does not have any relationship with the outside world in which they will be applying the concepts they are learning. Instead, by using a variety of authentic real-world applications, students have the ability to apply skills and knowledge to something that is tangible and meaningful to them.

Such assignments can include group work or individual work, discussions, graphical analysis, reflections, or even tests and quizzes. There are a few specific keys to developing successful performance assessments. Each of these assignments occurs over time; detailed and timely feedback is given at the end of each task so that students gain a feeling of how they are progressing through the course. The best way to grade each assignment, once you have decided upon the criteria, is using a rubric that states the criteria clearly and concisely so that the students are fully aware of the requirements for proficiency. Make sure that the standards being assessed have been identified and are clear and achievable and the directions for the task are clear and understood by the students.

Identify Desired Results

As with other professions, national, state, district, or institutional standards inform and shape our work and can serve as a guide for assessment design. At the beginning of your course, you should have gone through and asked yourself, "What do I want the students to know and be able to do after their time spent in this course?" Only when you have assessed for yourself what the outcomes will be will you be able to design both your formative and your summative assessment pieces. It is important to have clear and achievable standards to follow. If criteria and standards are known in advance, they can help guide the students' work. By identifying these standards, it will make your job as an instructor easier as well as make it easier to write the assessments and the rubrics that assess these standards. Performance tasks do not always have one correct answer; there are usually many ways in which a student may successfully complete them; this will become apparent if you allow the students to be as creative as they can. Performance assessment for projects needs to be open ended, real and multifaceted. Using rubrics to score your students work will make it easier as long as you have well-defined criteria for proficiency.

Following is a sample of some course objectives that were drawn from a master's course in technology and learning.

After the course, students should be able to:

- Expand personal definitions and examples of pedagogy and the psychology of learning with technology in a constructivist manner.
- Reflect on personal learning and contrast viewpoints on learning and development.
- Understand how learning is influenced by individual experience, talent, and prior learning, as well as language, culture, family, and community values.
- Learn to use new software.

- Support the work of classmates and participate in class discussions.
- Structure learning through intellectually challenging computer-based projects.
- Design and demonstrate the acquisition of new technological fluency in telecommunications and multimedia projects that provide opportunities for students to use technology as a tool, medium, and setting for learning via the Web.
- Create a digital portfolio of your work and learning in an area of inquiry chosen by the student.
- Perform and display your own educational technology projects.
- Develop an awareness of what journals and scholars relate to this field, technology resources, and services available to educators.

Outcomes and Evidence

After you have determined the standards and desired results for your course, you then have to identify what will be sufficient evidence for which your students can show their proficiency for the standards. This evidence should be more than just one summative multiple-choice test at the end of the course or unit. It should enable the students to apply and demonstrate higher-level thinking and complex reasoning skills that would not be possible with a multiple-choice or fact-memorization test. Ideally, students should be given a choice of what format their end product will take, but for all students the measured outcomes of success and the criteria on which they are judged will be consistent and the same. Successful outcomes serve as a tool to legitimize the innovative instructional strategies in our online program.

Clearly Written Directions

It is key that any directions or instructions you give to your students for an assignment, be it formative or summative assessment, are clear, concise, and to the point. Nothing causes confusion more for students than instructions that are contradictory or hard to follow. Be sure to use language that everyone understands, not just language familiar only to those who are comfortable with your individual style or are in the same field as you. The use of slang or specific terms used in the fields might be misunderstood by a student who is new to the course material. Run through both the assignment instructions and the accompanying rubric with the students in an online chat session for clarification and to make sure that everyone understands what is required. It might also be beneficial to create a thread in the asynchronous discussion area specifically for questions and concerns on specific assignments. We like having the students restate expectations and have them rewrite the rubric or even having the instructor write it with the students guiding the process so that all of the instructor's goals are assessed as well as some student goals. This type of interaction about expectations leaves the students feeling empowered and with a very clear idea of what is expected. You might also wish to create an online glossary for the students to reference in case they are unsure of what certain terminology means. Another way of checking your instructions would be to have a former student go over them and check for understanding.

FEEDBACK

There are some profoundly exciting ways for students to demonstrate their knowledge, skills, and learning through technology and for the instructor to provide students with meaningful feedback. Students are looking for how the instructor is reading their contributions, if their participation is valued, and if their participation is adequate in terms of quantity and quality. The presence of the instructor helps to keep the group on task. Whole-class commentary has been found to be satisfactory from the student point of view. Not all feedback has to be individual. Even though the communication among the group is to be kept free flowing and flexible, the instructor still maintains the "path" of the course with timely quality feedback for both the individual and the group. It is key to remember that the feedback does not have to be individualized to be effective but instead it must happen in a timely manner. Do not leave all your feedback until the end of the unit, after which it is too late for students to make adjustments to the quality of their work. Using the formative assessments you develop along the way will provide you with the opportunity to provide feedback to your students at checkpoints throughout the course. By providing constant and meaningful comments to your students, you allow them the opportunity to reflect on their own practices.

Encourage your students to give peer reviews of one another's work as they make their way through the course. Sometimes it is easier for a student to take criticism from a classmate than from the instructor. Students working in groups can provide one another with valuable information and insight before a final project is due. Allowing students to work together and have constructive dialogue enhances the quality of the learning that is happening in your course. Being critical consumers of peers work increases the students' understanding for themselves and those they are providing the feedback for. It's a double dip!

It is not recommended that points be given for quantity of responses in asynchronous and synchronous discussions, as this seems to make the discussion mechanical and not cognitive. The feedback should be allowed to focus on quality. We encourage that attendance and time spent are not as important, but rather the priority is the learning outcomes. Look at the content; look at what kind of thought the students have put into their feedback to you. Find out if they are applying the ideas from the course resources somewhere by listening to their outcomes. This will build better learning skills for your students. From the very beginning of the course, stress that posts and commentary in both asynchronous and synchronous settings need to reflect quality and not quantity. This will most likely evolve over time as a group norm, but it is important to quickly bring the group to the conclusion that the dialogue you are looking to see adds to the learning experience. Quickly stop irrelevant, personal posts by stressing that assessment is based on quality thoughtful dialogue that adds to the learning experience.

Here are some examples of threaded discussion feedback to the group:

Hello Everyone,

Okay, I am pleased to say that I've looked through the threaded discussion, and I'm happy with the topics each of you has chosen for your first project. They are due February 15. You will need to publish your project to the Web and post the URL in the "Projects" thread so your colleagues and I can offer you positive comments and suggestions for improvement. I will ask you to provide detailed feed-

back on at least two other classmate's projects in threaded discussion
the week after they have been posted. I want us to build the educational processes online so everyone can see and evaluate what is being created.

Please include a section on your Web page for this project where
you will share your insights beyond what you have already done in
the past with curriculum design. I will have time this week in the
synchronous session to discuss any questions or ideas. For additional
information and questions, please feel free to email or call me.

I am very pleased with the contributions and leadership thus far.
Thanks
Prof. M——

and

Everyone,
Friendly reminder . . .

You all need to offer positive comments and suggestions for improvement on other classmates' projects. They are eagerly waiting.
I know—they have told me. I am asking you to provide detailed
feedback on at least two other classmates' projects in our threaded
discussion area. After your colleagues and I have responded, we
will further discuss them in a later synchronous session. I will give
feedback on this assignment via email related to your creativity, coherent reflection, and practical relevance. I am hoping to get your
grades and feedback to you by next week.

For additional information and questions, please feel free to
email or call me.

Example: Individual Feedback

Hi T——

I have sent three messages now looking for the small project
that was due Feb 25. Just wanted to offer some feedback on your
progress in our —— class. students.pepperdine.edu/xxxx/omet/

I have been periodically checking your Web page that lists the
courses. So far I have not been able to find a link to your small

project. Please send a link to where I can locate the small project by [insert date and time].

In threaded discussion you have not begun to work cooperatively to develop ideas and interpretations of class content. I do not as of yet see logic and evidence in your contributions.

You have not provided evidence of a growing awareness of course content in threaded discussions or demonstrated an understanding and application of the process of using technology in class discussion. In addition, in threaded discussions and synchronous sessions, you need to explore and examine specific tasks in which it might be useful for teaching or training in your workplace.

I have yet to see you gaining a sense of confidence and familiarity in using curricular concepts in planning to be exhibited in your small project. I hope to see more growth as you continue to adapt to other contexts so you can prepare trainees to use it in innovative ways.

As I mentioned in my email two weeks ago, you have an F for the project and an F for the participation piece of our class, as you only have one post to threaded discussion that I can find.

You still have time to get in threaded discussions and still potentially get a good grade for the course if you get on board in the discussions and try to have a presence now and send the small project within 48 hours, after which I will not accept it.

Hello K——

This is the halfway point for the term. I wanted to give you a heads-up notice that I feel you are not doing well in our ——course this trimester. This is due to failure to attend our synchronous discussion session, failure to participate fully in threaded discussion, and missing or late journal entries and follow up on one-page summary from our midpoint meeting. I think it is only fair to allow you an opportunity to bring up your grade, but I must hear from you. I know your life is busy, but you have also made a commitment to this program. Perhaps you are not aware that your grade is now in danger. Let me hear from you.

Sincerely,

Professor's name

Hi J——

Just wanted to offer you some feedback on your progress in our —— class.

Your new-hire model is an interesting evaluation. I doubt many people consider the fact that a three-month probationary period is another way of saying "you are good enough" rather than an opportunity to say "how you can grow into this job." We have all had a new job where we were not quite certain how to handle every aspect. You bring up the good point that supervisors do not always understand fully or appreciate how a position relates to other employees.

You might want to reconsider rewriting the bullet regarding flat organizational structure. It is not clear what you mean by "flat" organizational structure. It is also confusing what you mean by direct reports to department heads and/or deans rather than interest of bosses. What's confusing here is if you're referring to intrusive bosses as a personality type or function. After all, isn't a department head a boss? Also, it's not clear what you mean by the degree of autonomy is subject to supervisors' personality and opportunity for advancement.

Overall I think that your report would have benefited by weaving the bullets into a stronger narrative. It is sometimes difficult to be clear about exactly what you are trying to say. The color coding definitely helps but doesn't overcome this one obstacle. Beyond the presentation, your insight is good and demonstrates that you understand what it means to be a participant in a community.

Please add these items above if they exist time permits and send me an update. Then I will revise you to an A from an A- on this project.

In both the synchronous and asynchronous discussions you have worked cooperatively to develop ideas and interpretations of class content. I see logic and evidence in your contributions.

You have provided evidence of a growing awareness of course content and demonstrated an understanding and application of the process using technology. In addition, you have thought of specific tasks in which it might be useful for teaching or training in your workplace. You are gaining a sense of confidence and familiarity in using curricular concepts in planning, too. I hope to see more growth as you continue to adapt to other contexts, so you can pre-pare trainees to use it in innovative ways.

Keep up the good work

You have an A- for the project and an A for the class so far.

And another example below of individual feedback

Course #, title, and instructor
Name: Student
Required Tasks
Homepage: Clear design sense, so crisp and clean. I wish more of the Web had some design sense about it.

Small-Group Activity: You contributed to the Web page design but I would have liked to have seen your presence in the content, too—leadership and a write-up reflecting your group discussion around the Web site content, and development of the Web page with your group's results.

Readings/Computer Store: I don't see any evidence in threaded discussion or from your homepage that you did read Tapscott. You have one good posting on one of the online documents, but that's it. You don't present or discuss the computer-store experience or engage in discussion of the Web sites that were listed on the syl-labus. In one of the chat sessions you do make it clear that you vis-ited the FairTest site and even engaged in discussion about it with someone at work, but you don't offer any thoughts about it to your classmates. It's not clear what role, if any, you had in the large group/community homepage construction. You aren't there as a participant in the discussion of it.

Participation
Threaded Discussions: You have only seven postings, and several of those are logistical rather than substantive. I don't see you en-gaged with your colleagues or me in discussion.

Chat: You are so animated and tuned in when you're in chat. I wish I could get that same person to interact in newsgroups. You can't rely on "chat" as participation in this program. Chat isn't the best venue for deep thoughts or extended discourse.

Course Grade

C Given your extremely minimal threaded-discussion participation, C is your grade. It puts you on academic probation.

The Role of Feedback in Final Evaluations

Posting or giving feedback in chat to the large group is also an effective strategy for motivating and reassuring students. Pay careful attention to comments from students. If it seems that they might be frustrated or do not participate as often as others, address it immediately and individually, to keep the course and the student on track. Activities need to tie in assessed learning objectives; if not; students will quickly become discouraged and uninterested. The conversation will move off focus and into topics that are not even course related. This will become frustrating for the members of the group who want to stay on task and further their learning by discussion of the academic topic at hand. The theory of collaboration is based on the fact that members of the community work with one another. Encourage students to keep one another on track by providing peer feedback. One idea spins out of another. If the discussion is not related to reading, project, or course content, it will be very difficult for the community to be able to be effective in exploring the course concepts.

Give general feedback and a feel for where your students are at different times during the course. Encourage peers to give feedback, which is why all coursework and URL links are posted on the threaded discussions newsgroup. Also, since many projects are team projects, take into account the various input from all team members before giving final grades on group projects.

For synchronous sessions, we tend to note only attendance unless someone's input during a session is stellar. Sometimes this varies depending on the way the chat session is conducted (e.g., students are responsible for the session). For threaded discussion, we have a rubric and rate from exceeding standards, meeting standards, and not meeting standards. The rubric is outlined on the syllabus. We try to keep some record of the quality of their contributions and responses. We try to note flashes of brilliance, and we try to always remember to make notes when we read the transcripts after the real-time session. We see that students take fewer notes (in class). They rely on the lectures and discussions being available online, and they do more than just listen in class; instead they "hear" what we are saying. We also try to give written feedback midcourse, but it is hard to guess what they will do since many major assignments are due at the end of the course.

Overall, we really prefer to give students written feedback along the way. We do this via email and sometimes on threaded discussions. Also, tell students that you hope that they move beyond grades in this program. Our whole goal is to help them realize that understanding is more important than grades. While we have to have some deadlines and grades, more importantly, we want to help guide the students to an understanding that can continue beyond the end of one course and into the next.

Be very clear that you are expecting students to move beyond "cocktail-party knowledge." They are reading and reflecting, expanding their thoughts, ideas, and opinions, and they should be citing from readings and reflections from peers in the asynchronous and synchronous conversations. This will reinforce that the student is grasping the concepts you are teaching and can relate the course work to the subject matter or experience they are sharing. Look for originality and depth in each student's contribution or project.

As far as the immediate feedback aspect of getting test results quickly over the Internet, some instructors think this seems very superficial (in terms of getting results that really mean something). The argument goes, "Are we testing for information or knowledge here?" Most instructors use online testing more as a tool of progress and rely on written work in the course as a larger or more significant form of assessment. Some instructors may want more qualitative, narrative, and deeper feedback. I can assess via the Net if someone has truly internalized the concepts and is not just memorizing by looking at applications of concepts in discussions and projects. This is a strategy we use to reliably grade an essay for something more than misspellings and grammar. Some instructors teach a totally online performance-based course, for example, public-speaking-course students are then required to come to campus or another "space" to videotape three required speeches. While this is not a face-to-face meeting, some performance-type courses will require some additional creative means to meet course objectives.

At Pepperdine there is no online testing. All assessment is done by reviewing and analyzing the content in the assigned projects. Because many of the projects are so open ended, there is a great deal of critical thinking involved in order to accomplish the assigned goal. Not only is critical thinking involved, but the students get to show their creative side as well. If a project does not meet the requirements, the student is notified with some well-structured feedback to make some improvements before the end of the course or receive the current grade until the project can be improved.

ASSESSING THE STUDENT

Rubrics

By clearly defining the course expectations, you are establishing a structure for formal assessment. The most effective way to make the course requirements clear is to create a rubric or checklist, listing specific criteria for satisfactory performance. Assessment engages students directly in the evaluation of their own work and can help make content connections clear. Rubrics can be expressed in frameworks and standards. Successful integration of content learning requires projects to be based on standards, to have clearly articulated goals, and to support and demonstrate content learning both in process and product. Make sure the rubric clearly distinguishes three or four levels of performance and that each assignment or assessment piece addresses multiple intelligences. It may be important in assessment design to align course goals with new local and national standards or proficiencies as they emerge in your workplace. The products and presentations that our students do are clear outcomes for knowledge. Rubrics are made to establish standards so students have knowledge of our expectations and set parameters for student endeavors. Projects have the potential to clarify the purpose of learning for students. There are thousands of Web sites that provide teachers with pre-made rubrics in any number of subject areas. Ultimately, however, the most useful rubrics are those you create yourself. A rubric can range from a detailed four-level analysis of each standard to a simple check-off list of required components for an assignment.

We have found that rubrics have increased our student performance because they perform better knowing their goal upfront. Rubrics provide greater coherence, which equals greater performance achievement and, in turn, informs them and helps shape their work into effective displays of student knowledge and learning. Scoring guided by rubrics for individual tasks, group work, and major assignments helps the learner make the connection between standards and assessments. These assignments can become personal in choice for the topic of a specific task. I also like having students score themselves according to the rubric sometime before or as the project is handed in; it seems to add more meaning and understanding. Sometimes the assignments are scored using a rubric by an individual course instructor, peers in the course, a course mentor, or a group of faculty. In some cases, a validating group made up of community and university members can be used to score the assignment, such as the end-of-course exhibition model that we use.

Designing a Rubric

After you have identified the course standards and the assignments that you will use for your course, you will need to create the rubrics that determine the criteria for a student to show that they have been successful in applying their knowledge and skills to the assignment topic. Start with an exemplary project, what you would expect the best project to look like, and then identify the key elements of this exemplary project. Be specific in what you determine exemplary and what you consider proficient. Use terms that are specific to the degree of proficiency you desire, and do not use subjective terms such as "knows," which can cause students confusion. By using a rubric, you can ensure that all students are on the same page and that grading is not subjective or skewed due to personal biases or feelings. Rubrics can be very time consuming to create and develop. However, once you have constructed a rubric for the first time and used it and made adjustments, you can use it again with other assignments by tweaking it as necessary depending on the criteria for the task. A basic four-point rubric can look like the following:

4. Clear, well-developed thesis that details in a sophisticated fashion with [key] components.
3. Clear, developed thesis that deals with [key issues].
2. General thesis responding to all components superficially.
1. Little or no analysis.

(Educational Testing Service/College Board, 1992, 25)

Bloom's Taxonomy

Benjamin Bloom (1967) created this taxonomy for categorizing the level of abstraction of questions that commonly occur in educational settings. The taxonomy provides a useful structure in which to categorize test questions, since professors will characteristically ask questions within particular levels. If you can determine the levels of questions that will appear on your exams, you will be able to guide your students using appropriate strategies. Using these categories and cues, you can create challenging and open-ended projects for your students. The words used by Bloom to describe the competencies are valuable when writing rubrics, as they provide language that is clear and specific for your instructions.

Competence - Skills Demonstrated

Knowledge

- Observation and recall of information.
- Knowledge of dates, events, and places.
- Knowledge of major ideas.
- Mastery of subject matter.
- Question cues: list, define, tell, describe, identify, show, label, collect, examine, tabulate, quote, name, who, when, and where.

Comprehension

- Understanding information.
- Grasp meaning.
- Translate knowledge into new context.
- Interpret facts, compare, and contrast.
- Order, group, and infer causes.
- Predict consequences.
- Question cues: summarize, describe, interpret, contrast, predict, distinguish, estimate, differentiate, discuss, and extend.

Application

- Use information.
- Use methods, concepts, and theories in new situations.

- Solve problems using required skills or knowledge.
- Question cues: apply, demonstrate, calculate, illustrate, show, solve, examine, modify, relate, change, classify, experiment, and discover.

Analysis

- Seeing patterns.
- Organization of parts.
- Recognition of hidden meanings.
- Identification of components.
- Question cues: analyze, separate, order, explain, connect, classify, arrange, divide, compare, select, explain, and infer.

Synthesis

- Use old ideas to create new ones.
- Generalize from given facts.
- Relate knowledge from several areas.
- Predict and draw conclusions.
- Question cues: combine, integrate, modify, rearrange, plan, create, design, invent, "what if?", compose, formulate, prepare, generalize, and rewrite.

Evaluation

- Compare and discriminate between ideas.
- Assess value of theories and presentations.
- Make choices based on reasoned argument.
- Verify value of evidence.
- Recognize subjectivity.
- Question cues: assess, decide, rank, grade, test, measure, recommend, convince, select, judge, explain, discriminate, support, conclude, compare, and summarize.

Rubrics need continual adjustment in their working to allow prospective sharing, revisions, and help in making them most effective.

In an online collaborative environment, rubrics can be somewhat flexible. Included below are rubrics used by online instructors in the Pepperdine model. Assessment directions need to be clearly written as noted with the examples provided below.

Sample: Instructions and Rubric for Journal Assignments

You will keep a journal. Excerpts from it will show up in our discussion. Weekly accounts from you will be sent to me via email attachments or html files. Keeping a journal as you complete this class will help you sort your thoughts, reflect on what you are learning, and hopefully lead you to further inquiries about your study. The following is a rubric to guide you in completing journal entries:

- Ideas are well developed (at least a full paragraph).
- Writing can be either formal or informal (personal musings or more structured comments).
- Evidence of critical thinking.
- Email me link included on journal page for instructor and peer feedback.
- Journals are submitted in a timely fashion.

Sample: Rubric for project Web pages and/or digital portfolio

- Subject matter is accurate.
- Applies current instructional principles.
- Project is appropriate to learning outcomes.
- Content is appropriate to level of student.
- Presentation is grammatically correct.
- Presentation is visually appealing (need to ensure that the concepts and procedures are conveyed well graphically).
- Presentation flow is logical.
- Reflection integrates learning experience with ideas for the course readings and discussions.
- Email link included to allow for instructor feedback and comments from peers.

One of the major assessments in the Pepperdine model is the Action Research Project (ARP), which is presented both online in the student's portfolio and as an exit exhibition. Below is a sample rubric for the exhibition:

Exhibition Rubric Sample:
  I. Organizational Qualities

4. The presentation tells the story of the ARP. The observer can figure out what the student did and what he or she found out. Display is clear, easy to follow, clearly labeled, well designed, error free, visually appealing, and includes important milestones and events.
1. The presentation is badly executed. It is difficult to determine what the student did, why, and what happened; materials are not well marked; the presentation lacks a theme or organizing element; construction of the display is sloppy; and materials contain errors.

  II. Linkage to Program

4. The presentation gives evidence of linkage to the "big ideas" of the course in the program. It is apparent that the student made use of course work in the Action Research Project.
1. The presentation gives little evidence of relation to the program. Few course ideas, if any, are apparent in the work. The presentation suggests that the Action Research Project could have occurred independently of the MA program.

  III. Evidence of Data-based Reflection

4. The presentation contains evidence that the student made periodic, thoughtful reconsideration of work underway based upon his or her consideration of data from the endeavor (e.g., notes, documents, conversations, video tapings, and so on).
1. The presentation gives the impression that the project moved on without periodic, thoughtful reconsideration or

that modifications in the project are not based upon data analysis but upon intuition or guesswork. There is no evidence that the student gathered information or made use of gathered information.

IV. Evidence of Synthesis of Data

4. The presentation has evidence of systematic synthesis of data; the student pulled information together from a variety of sources to make decisions and make sense of his or her ARP. There is evidence the student has triangulated information (looked at multiple points of view on the same point).
1. The presentation does not reference information from more than one or two sources. The student has not attempted to extract and consider feedback or input from critical friends, tutors, participants in the ARP, documents, materials, notes, or other sources.

V. Responsiveness to Oral Questioning

4. The student is able to answer questions about project implementation, about problems and their resolution during the ARP, and about his/her conclusions or insights. The student's answers reference course content.
1. The student has difficulty responding to probing questions about project implementation, about problems and their resolution during the ARP, about his or her conclusions or insights. The student's answers are not anchored in reasoning related to ideas in the program.

And finally, here is a grading sample that we use sometimes when we talk about the requirements of our face-to-face meetings for our online program:

To receive credit you must complete all assignments to meet the criteria below and participate fully online and face to face.
There are only three (3) face-to-face meetings.

a. If you miss a face-to-face meeting, you will not pass the course.

b. If your postings are total less than one standard deviation of the average number of postings, you will not receive credit (e.g., if the average is 40 and the SD is 8, you need to have 32 or more postings).

c. Postings should be distributed throughout the semester, not piled on at the end. Postings should move the conversation forward, not simply agree with prior postings or share URLs without relevant commentary.

d. You will not receive credit if your team members report that you did not carry your weight, did not complete the work you agreed to do, or did a horrible job, requiring revision by other team members.

e. You will not receive credit if your personal Web page is not complete, ignores WWW protocol, doesn't function properly, or if you have problems assembling it on the designated server.

Interactive Requirements

When developing your assessment requirements, build in an area for participation in formal and informal activities. This will include your students' participation in both the synchronous and the asynchronous environments. Some ideas for you to consider when building in some interactive synchronous resources into your course are:

- Distributed Collaborators (e.g., group members and expert resources at a distance).
- Web-Based Inquiry. How do I know what we know?
- Case Application. Illustrative inquiry units and/or scenarios with concrete examples of how to apply concepts.
- Rich Media.
- Public Demonstration of Learning. Web-based portfolio using graphics, sound, and video.

As an instructor for online learners in small groups, I have learned that students find using the chat-room feature very helpful in planning, organizing, and reviewing ideas for small-group projects. Upon request, our group leader or instructor can send group members a copy of his or her chat transcript, which often proves to be a great tool in accomplishing what we had discussed. Using this transcript, an instructor can determine the amount of participation that each group member put out and allow the instructor to gauge the level of commitment from each student in a project.

Following are some sample participation guidelines for participation and informal activities that you might wish to share with your students:

- Participation.

  Participation does not mean showing up, although this is a minimal requirement. Participation means posting meaningful contributions in threaded discussions, interacting during online discussions, engaging in activities and tasks, and helping your classmates outside the required meeting times. In this particular course, helping your cohort buddies is paramount. Working through ideas with classmates helps break the stereotype that communicating about course work, sources, and project ideas is cheating. Assessment involves not only how much you participate in threaded discussions and online discussion but also what the quality of interaction is among others in the group. Formal activities are described in the syllabus, albeit thinly for now. Expect all formal work to be published to the Net (available from one's homepage), and it is reasonable to require all Net-published work done for the class to exhibit good writing and accurate spelling and grammar. As in all academic settings, plagiarism is not to be tolerated and should be grounds for expulsion from the course and/or program; this includes images and sounds as well as words. Get permission. Cite fully.

  For groups, we hate it when one student messes up a group project. But we really have no sympathy for group members who shoulder the work that the slacker has left to them and then complain about it. Share with students that you, the instructor, are very happy to mediate group process if need be. But first, handle your group. Have due dates for checking up on work-in-progress. Check in with your class regularly. Ask if someone's having trouble, and ask it in a way that lets that person 'fess up and get help in a timely fashion.

- Informal Activities.

     These are the little tasks or chores that we ask our students to carry out in the name of learning. Usually these arise on the fly from something that has transpired in threaded discussion or chat. Just-in-time piece—often monitoring and adjusting the learning activities and direction of your teaching to meet student needs and current events. Sometimes it could be just a notion that pops up from whatever related outside work you're engaged in at the time. These are not time fillers. Take them seriously and respond to them insightfully when they arise.

TECHNOLOGY PIECE EVALUATION

A main component of the Pepperdine model for our online courses is the use of technology to investigate and display the concepts being taught. The main learning processes in this course are via project work and reflection on that work; specifically, doing something and thinking about it with others and alone. Learning is most effectively accomplished with the help of others, though the student will be graded as an individual. All the project work and reflections will be displayed on the Web in the form of a digital portfolio.

We encourage our students to select an area of inquiry and design a plan to explore and exhibit newfound learning. The students should play to their strengths and not leave the hardest work to the last minute. The best work done in our courses has been created by students who embraced the opportunity to learn something new. No topic is too crazy. Previous projects have included simulation design, digital poetry, music composition, artificial intelligence, virtual worlds, multimedia, digital video production, global information systems, video conferencing, and animation.

The three big ideas of this course are:

- Construct
- Reflect
- Exhibit

Creativity, intellectual rigor, and innovation are highly valued! Each student will choose an area of inquiry that all course work, with the exception of assigned readings and classroom tutorials, will revolve around. An area of inquiry should be deep and broad enough for a student to demonstrate new learning and provide opportunity for rich exploration and construction.

Chosen areas should be fields, topics, or disciplines already changed and/or enhanced by technology or could be in ways developed by a student. Several pieces of software should be mastered and evaluated in relation to the chosen area of inquiry. Your students may know something about an area of inquiry or have a significant interest in that topic, but they still have room for growth. All of their work, thoughts, products, logs, and discovered digital resources will be assembled in a digital portfolio on the World Wide Web. They should be adding to this portfolio throughout the course. Have students complete a learning blueprint and have it signed, digitally of course, by you. Have them plan their work, jotting down the due dates of their project selections and major milestones in their completion. Include other major obligations that might impinge on your course work from outside this course. Have students add a completed calendar of events to their course blueprint.

Using Web Portfolios for Assessments

In addition to synchronous and asynchronous online discussions, Pepperdine students are also given the responsibility of creating, building, and maintaining their own Web site. Portfolios were mentioned earlier in this chapter, but since this piece is very unique to the Pepperdine model, we thought that we should describe it further. Since one of the challenges of online learning is how to verify individual success, evaluating each student's Web portfolio is an efficient means of measuring student performance. It is a good idea for teachers to place projects in portfolios or on an educational file server for sharing with others—both in the course and globally over the Internet.

The emphasis of a student's Web site is placed on content, clarity, and usability rather than flashiness. As students move through their courses, they document their progress in narrative form accompanied with audio, graphics, and video. A good deal of journaling is required, which encourages students to reflect on the skills, knowledge, and practices that they have acquired from the program.

In evaluating both the contents and logistics of the Web portfolio, certain elements should be required. Examples of those are:

- Email me links on each page that will allow both the instructor and peers to send feedback to the student.
- Easy navigation throughout the site. Examples: buttons and title bars.
- Design sense of Web pages—using a consistent design throughout the site.
- Need to ensure that the concepts and procedures are conveyed graphically.
- Appropriate use of detailed bullets, numbered bullets, and sentences.
- Formats compression and plug-ins linked to page needed to view student projects.
- Display the Web tracks for research projects (path taken).
- "Responsible Resource Use" format for citing Web sites.

Below we have outlined the requirements for successfully completing the digital portfolio portion of our Pepperdine course, as well as how heavily each section is weighted. Please remember that this is just a guide and is not set in stone. Use creativity and freedom when planning your course to suit not only your needs but the needs of your students.

1. Construct (25% of portfolio grade)
   Constructionism is a participatory sport. Students should use a computer to construct a project that requires effort, creativity, and persistence. This project should help students learn more about their topic of inquiry through the active exploration of a problem or set of problems.
2. Reflect (20% of portfolio grade)
   Students should collect resources, read materials related to the field, be reflective in their practice, and demonstrate an understanding of their newly acquired knowledge in online discussions and projects. It is assumed that digital and traditional materials will be used for research purposes.

3. Exhibit (20% of portfolio grade)

   All of your work should be assembled in a digital online WWW portfolio. This portfolio should include your construction (via screen shots if no online plug-in is available), sketches from your design notebooks, online resources used by you and related to your area of inquiry, links to related materials, logs of salient online communications, thoughts about what you learned about the area of inquiry, reflections on your learning, and reviews of software packages used. The final portfolio should be well organized and visually attractive and make a contribution to the world of ideas.

4. Apply (10% of portfolio grade)

   Students should use a few different pieces of software related to their area of inquiry. You should be able to compare and contrast the ease of use, applicability, and flexibility of the software packages. Some constructions will require the use of several different software packages. The more open ended the package, the better for your students to work constructively. Packages such as StarLogo, Microworlds, Tabletop, Stella, graphics packages, Geometer's Sketchpad, Interactive Physics, and musical sequencers are types of software I have in mind. Of course, basic tool software counts, but not too much! Reflections on learning these new packages should be included in your portfolio.

5. Join (5% of portfolio grade)

   Students should find an online community of practice and/or professional organization dedicated to your area of inquiry. You should participate in this community and record your interactions for inclusion in your portfolio.

6. Teach (10% of portfolio grade)

   Share a piece of your project or ask a student or colleague to solve a problem related to your construction. Record your interactions and reflect upon the teaching and/or learning that occurs.

7. Write to an expert (10% of portfolio grade)

   After doing some of the readings, you might want to write to an expert in the thinking skill, cooperative learning, or technology arena. For instance, you might write to someone who has developed a unique thinking skill program or cooperative learning technique in your state. You also might want to see what else exists on a topic, find out how teachers are using a software program, write to competing researchers for research reports, or something similar. It is the exploratory, inquisitive nature of the task that is prized here, not what you actually do. You must post on the Web a three-page summary of what you did, why you chose this activity, what you expect to gain from it, any resources received, and send a copy of your letter(s) via email to me.

After you have established these sections, you will then need to create a rubric that accompanies the assignment.

It is important to stress to your students the need to assess sources carefully and be responsible for their use when attaching them to their own Web portfolios. The following format for citing Web sites is very valuable to share with your students:

1. Author's name (if known) (last name, first name)
2. The full title of the work in quotation marks.
3. The title of the complete work, if applicable, in italics.
4. The document date if known and if different from the date accessed.
5. The full http address.
6. The date of visit.

EXHIBITION

The final exhibition is a chance for the student to demonstrate what they have learned online during the last face-to-face meeting. The student must be able to connect what he or she has learned to what they are presenting to the panel of faculty. The exhibition rubric in figure 5.4 is a sample of what the student is expected to be able to do as a result of his or her experience in our community of practice. During these few days, as shown in the sample schedule figure 5.5, students will spend time finishing their course work and giving an oral presentation, supplemented by a visual display and their artifacts from the year.

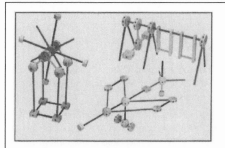

I. Organizational Qualities

4—The presentation tells the story of the ARP. The observer can figure out what the student did and what s/he found out. Display is clear, easy to follow, includes important milestones/events; clearly labeled; neatly executed design; error free; visually appealing.

1—The presentation is badly executed. It is difficult to determine what the student did, why, and what happened; materials are not well marked; the presentation lacks a theme or organizing element; construction of the display is sloppy, materials contain errors.

II. Linkage to Program

4—The presentation gives evidence of linkage to the 'big ideas' of the course in the program. It is apparent that the student made use of coursework in the action research project.

1—The presentation gives little evidence of relation to the program. Few course ideas, if any, are apparent in the work. The presentation suggests that the ARP could have occurred independently of the MA program.

III. Evidence of Data-based Reflection

4—The presentation contains evidence that the student made periodic, thoughtful reconsideration of work underway, based upon her/his consideration of data from the endeavor, eg., notes, documents, conversations, video tapings, and so on.

1—The presentation gives the impression that the project moved on without periodic, thoughtful reconsideration, or that modifications in the project were not based upon data analysis but upon intuition or guesswork. There is no evidence that the student gathered information or made use of gathered information.

IV. Evidence of Synthesis of Data

4—The presentation has evidence of systematic synthesis of data; the student pulled information together from a variety of sources to make decisions and make sense of his/her ARP. There is evidence the student has triangulated information (looked at multiple points of view on the same point).

1—The presentation does not reference information from more than one or two sources. The student has not attempted to extract and consider feedback or input from critical friends, tutors, participants in the ARP, documents, materials, notes, or other sources.

Figure 5.4.   *OMAET Rubric*

(continued)

V. Responsiveness to Oral Questioning

4—The student is able to answer questions about project implementation, about problems and their resolution during the ARP, about her/his conclusions, or insights. The student's answers reference course content.

1—The student has difficulty responding to probing questions about project implementation, about problems and their resolution during the ARP, about her/his conclusions, or insights. The student's answers are not anchored in reasoning related to ideas in the program.

Figure 5.4. (continued)

Program Assessments and Evaluation

It is always prudent to ask your students to provide you with feedback at the end of your course or program. You can also focus on how well students are representing different perspectives. You might fill in the missing perspectives or have students review their work and identify missing perspectives. At the end of the course you might wish to send your students an evaluation form for them to fill out about their experiences in the course. Here is a sample one that we like to use:

July 9–13, 2002
Final F2F for Cohort 4
Exhibitions

TENTATIVE Schedule of Activities

	9:00–2:00	LUNCH	1:00–3:30	4:00–5:00
TU				Meet in cohort groups with mentor. Fill out course evaluations; Financial Aid exit interviews
WE	ED 668 with Instructor CD Burning; Closure	On your own	ED 667 with Instructor Prep for Program Debrief; Closure	All Cohort Beach cookout??
TH	ED 630 with Instructor Next steps; Closure	On your own	Set up for Exhibitions	Dinner hosted by Pepperdine at Exhibitions Hall
FR	Exhibitions for Faculty Review	On your own	**Exhibitions Open to Public Hors d'oeuvres Hosted**	
SA	Graduation brunch- students & faculty only Speaker! Awards! Fun!		Program Debrief / Future Search /Open Space; Snacks provided	
SU	OPTIONAL Trip to Local Sites			

Figure 5.5. Final Meeting Schedule

Course Evaluation Form - <u>Mercedes Fisher</u>

I am happy that you participated in and successfully completed my course. I am now interested in your opinions, ideas, and experiences regarding my teaching and your learning. Please take a few minutes to complete the following survey.

Course: ☐ Cadre ☐

Please enter your responses and after you have completed the survey press the SUBMIT button at the end of this page. If you need to start all over, press the RESET THIS FORM button to clear the questionnaire. NOTE: Before you start to fill out the survey, please check that the SUBMIT button is visible at the bottom of this form. Sometimes the buttons at the bottom do not get loaded properly. If this is the case, please reload/refresh this page until they are visible.

1. Goals and objectives of this course were clear? ☐ Yes ☐ No

2. The instructor created a climate and established circumstances conducive to on-line learning? ☐ Yes ☐ No

3. Course had helpful readings, resources and assignments? ☐ Yes ☐ No

4. Course assignments are relevant and add to the learning experience? ☐ Yes ☐ No

5. I learned to understand important ideas in the course area better. ☐ Yes ☐ No

6. Given the nature of the course, the workload demands of the course were realistic. ☐ Yes ☐ No

7. Instructor increased my interest in the subject matter. ☐ Yes ☐ No

8. Instructor evaluated my work in ways that were helpful to me. ☐ Yes ☐ No

9. Instructor was available and helpful outside of class. ☐ Yes ☐ No

10. Projects were useful. ☐ Yes ☐ No

11. Instructor presents material in an effective and informative way. ☐ Yes ☐ No

12. Instructor integrated practical applications into the course. ☐ Yes ☐ No

13. Instructor effectively monitored students' understanding of subject matter through questions and support. ☐ Yes ☐ No

14. Instructor displayed caring and sensitivity toward students. ☐ Yes ☐ No

Figure 5.6. *Course Evaluation Form*

(continued)

15. Instructor assigned work which required critical thinking. Yes No

16. Overall, the course instructor was an effective teacher. Yes No

17. I made substantial effort to learn in this course. Yes No

18. The instructor seemed interested in presenting the course material. Yes No

19. The number of TI sessions were sufficient. Yes No

20. The instructor was successful in the initial face-to face meeting for raising my comfort level for the course. Yes No

PART II

21. To assist me with future planning for this course, would you please list activities. assignments or experiences that were particularly helpful or meaningful. Thank You.

22. What suggestions, if any, do you have for improving the course.

23. Please check any of the following word or statements that describe what you think of me as your instructor.

organized	empowering	boring
ineffective	unfriendly	confident
lenient	effective	biased/one-sided
hard to understand	cold	poor sense of humor
knowledgeable	disorganized	nervous

Figure 5.6.

(continued)

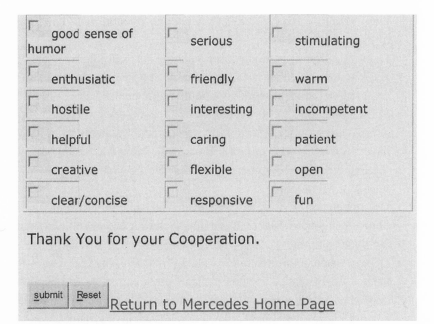

☐ good sense of humor	☐ serious	☐ stimulating
☐ enthusiatic	☐ friendly	☐ warm
☐ hostile	☐ interesting	☐ incompetent
☐ helpful	☐ caring	☐ patient
☐ creative	☐ flexible	☐ open
☐ clear/concise	☐ responsive	☐ fun

Thank You for your Cooperation.

submit   Reset   Return to Mercedes Home Page

Figure 5.6.   *(continued)*

You have now received the final feedback on [course number and name]. Please fill out the form below. I realize that many of you are busy. If a very brief answer to one or two of these questions is as much as you can manage, that will be valuable. The present shape of [name of program] has been determined to a large extent by the helpful feedback from earlier participants. Your feedback will be studied and taken into account in later courses I teach in the [name of program] program.

gsep.pepperdine.edu/~mmfisher/main/emailform.html

If you have any problems submitting this, please copy into a Word document and send to me. Thanks.

Appreciatively,

[Professor's Name]

For accreditation we have to demonstrate how our program meets the following standards:

• Clearly stated mission, educational goals, indicators of success, and assessment of program leadership. This standard also includes recruitment of diverse students, academic freedom, and handling of grievances.

- Demonstration of assessment of teaching and learning.
- Assignments, such as but not limited to, portfolios of various assessments of student work and faculty competence.
- Show graduation rates, evaluation by outside reviewers, and student focus groups. A follow-up survey with students after they have been out of the program for a while. Our documentation of the exhibits and the student portfolios on the Web are strong assessment documents.
- Documentation of resources that ensure sustainability (this includes library resources—especially online in our case—technology, and facilities/equipment).
- Demonstrated commitment to planning, plus learning and improvement. Documentation for this includes providing strategic-planning documents, documenting who has participated in the planning, using data for improvement, and collecting representative syllabi.

CONCLUSIONS

There is an interesting perception in education that somehow the way in which one structures assessment is completely different once we move learning online and out of the classroom, university lecture halls, and seminar rooms. When we first took the online program proposal to our accreditation body, we knew we'd get asked about that, and we were right. Mostly the questions were about authenticity of the students' work. How would we know Doug himself wrote the paper, did the project, or answered the essay questions? Of course the answer is, the same way you know it's Doug when he's in the face-to-face, traditional classroom. From interacting with Doug over the semester you have a sense of what he knows, what his syntax is like, and how he handles the ideas of the course that have come up in discussion. If there is a major discrepancy between that image of him and the image he projects in work he hands in, then you become suspicious and look more closely.

That answer satisfied the accreditation team and our faculty. However, as several students over the last few years brought to our attention, that is an answer for an old paradigm, a paradigm based on knowledge transmission as the detectable outcome of teaching and indicator of learning. They are correct in acknowledging that we are actually working a different paradigm. In a socio-cultural paradigm for learning, the outcome is best described as the transformation of identity, assuming that practice and identity are intertwined. When people learn in our program, we expect them to evolve, to become different people and, accordingly, to behave differently in situations based on newly accomplished understandings and capabilities. But that's at the end of the degree program. What are the intermediary steps (courses) and how are they assessed?

In our program, assessment is represented in the workplace and in the online program. The local workplace culture (e.g., teaching fifth grade in district X or managing corporate training for company Y), offers the student-participants ways of doing work—traditions, tools, language, colleagues, and so forth, essentially an authentic environment within which to learn. The online program offers a contradictory culture of learning. By making work, and talk about work, central in the program courses, we push students into that uncomfortable zone between worlds and support them in their efforts to reconcile those differences. In our program, the main assessment piece is an Action Research Project, which consists of a year-long project resulting in an online portfolio of student work and reflections on the student's Web site. The ARP affords the students the opportunity to reconcile the differences between the uncomfortable zones between worlds, with its cycles of effort, data collection, reflection, and repair. But, the courses also operate as mini-versions or en-route encounters with this same tension.

Students interact with one another, as well as faculty, workplace friends, and texts as they try to accomplish change in a piece of the workplace culture of practice. In several courses, instructors explicitly solicit documentation of the current workplace practices or personal operating beliefs (i.e., in a curriculum area). This task and its discussion in newsgroups illuminate current ways of doing things and the beliefs, tools, and intangibles that support those practices. Students then have a second project or second part to the task that asks them to apply an idea from the course to alter that practice.

CHAPTER 6

Conclusion

All significant breakthroughs were breaks with old ways of thinking.

—Thomas Kuhn, *The Structure of Scientific Revolutions*

Results show that students can learn concepts, skills, and demonstrate improved attitudes and achievement within an online context for instructors willing to invest the time in the aforementioned instructional strategies. Once your online courses are up and running, maintenance becomes an issue; first revise your course following its initial usage and subsequently each time you run it to update as needed. The ideas in this book are not the final answers, so you will need to revisit, revise, and update your course material as you move forward into the future of Web-based learning. Courses can continually be improved over many iterations as they are refined and modified. We suggest you frequently revisit your course structure to become familiar with what is working, what might need some adjustment, and what might need to be completely abandoned. We have provided a checklist as a guide for maintaining flexibility by allowing you to continue to meet the needs of many while also encouraging forward thinking.

COURSE MAINTENANCE CHECKLIST

Revisions to consider include but are not limited to:

- Update readings so they contribute a variety of outside resources (online and print based) in the hopes of building a knowledge base for the learner that is well rounded and up to date.

- Incorporate guest speakers and content experts as they become available.
- Align course goals with new local and national standards or proficiencies as they emerge in your workplace.
- Re-sequence activities if needed so the structure of online activity remains organized, purposeful, and on task.
- Continue to frame questions in terms of the concepts you want to remain focused on.
- Update logistics: dates, times and deadlines, and community or group name info for class group activities. Check for inconsistencies and/or inaccuracies in information that you present to your students. This ability to remain highly organized but appear effortlessly flexible will allow for the course to expand the opportunities for and expectations of learners. Good organization allows for flexibility!
- Conduct needs assessments to get a handle on your audience as course enrollment changes to include more diverse backgrounds, for example, corporate in typically K–12 settings.
- Check functionality of all links and Web-based resources, and update rubrics and checklists.
- Add new services as they evolve.
- Be willing to introduce new learner tools and capabilities as they emerge. When new resources present themselves, acknowledge them. As new technological capabilities emerge, the technology tools that you chose to use in your class should be re-examined to make sure they are the most appropriate and effective for the learning objectives you have set.

When you add changes, see how your students react. Ask students why they consider the assignment useful or not? Ask their thoughts for improvement. Seek counterparts who share your interest in online teaching. Discuss curricular and pedagogical issues with them, as this can support you as you progress with course revisions.

FIVE CHALLENGES FOR ONLINE LEARNING

The Internet has been touted as the ultimate agent of change in the workplace world. While that promise (or threat) has fallen notably flat in recent months, in at least one area its impact has been large and appears to be getting larger—Web-based learning. Changing the way instructors design and teach courses is not a simple process. The most challenging obstacle instructors will experience is their own fear of delving into the unknown. That is not to say that instructors are afraid of technology but of the consequences of technology. The Web presents a call to shift major paradigms about the ways in which learning takes place.

There are five major challenges of proactive application of online teaching and learning. Attention is given to ways in which teachers can help apply knowledge, awareness, and procedure to their own courses and successfully maximize the technology tools and their capabilities in their workplace.

Selectivity

There are politics and economics involved in preserving knowledge. Consider the money and time spent to digitize information. Do you ever wonder what has been left out in history and the impact its had on subsequent generations? Since money and time are limited resources, it is inevitable that some perspectives and details will be selectively left out. Even though the digital world enables a browser to spit out a hierarchy of sources on a topic, there is a limit to the amount of information we can explore, examine, and integrate effectively. Compounding the problem is the fact that students will learn only from the material they select. Subsequently, the students' knowledge base will expand and contract solely through the conduit of what the computer browser provides.

Malleability

The Digital Age allows data to be changed. "Morphing" is the new-age term that describes computer users' ability to take something and change it into something else. This method was most recently high-lighted in blockbuster movies such as *Jurassic Park* (wherein dinosaurs were brought back to life), *Forrest Gump* (wherein the fictional char-acter interacted with three dead presidents), and *The Matrix* (which introduced "bullet time" filming, where a photo was taken in 360 de-grees, and the resulting image could be rotated from any angle). These examples clearly exhibit the seductive and appealing power of digital media and the ease with which data can become so malleable and changeable. Thus, the ability to change things becomes almost an im-perative to do so. This is the empowerment provided by technology. However, it is done with potential social and psychological costs. When scenes are animated or reanimated and become realistic, younger children, adolescents, and some adults may wrestle with reality and fantasy. How many younger children thought dinosaurs were real after seeing *Jurassic Park* or that *Forrest Gump* was a part of history or that a person can stop bullets with the power of their mind? As educators and course designers, we have always rested in the notion of fact, ver-ifiability, and reality. New technology capabilities blur the distinctions between these three. Instructors at a minimum must avoid misleading students with unverifiable media, and in most or all courses it would be appropriate to include some work with information literacy and de-velop some goals on how to verify sources on Web sites as to whether they are fact or fiction.

Vulnerability

The excuses of the past, such as bogus "sick" days or "the dog ate my homework" are being replaced more and more often by "the server is down," "my hard drive crashed or was destroyed by a virus," or "I could not connect." In general, instructors tend to be very forgiving. The vulnerability that technology has created is both liberating and threatening in the sense that it expands students' capabilities as well as increases their dependence on technology. Also, from a knowledge standpoint, students are becoming increasingly dependent on those people who are proficient with technology. This vulnerability has cre-ated a new food chain in which most people are the plankton and peo-ple such as Microsoft's Bill Gates are great white sharks!

Exclusivity

Lots of students, instructors, and parents are not computer literate; therefore, they can become technophobic. This is a condition in which people are psychologically affected because they are not adequately equipped, economically or educationally, to utilize technology in their lives. It is not just a matter of the "have and have nots" but also the "can and cannots." The technophobes become the illiterate of the Information Age. For those who choose not to take part in technology, there is a danger of becoming completely irrelevant in that world. It is rapidly becoming a global problem, particularly in the marketplace (e.g., job security) when some workers know things others don't know.

Superficiality

Consider the information to which we have access. As with cable TV, there is often not a lot of substance on the Internet. Akin to a small village in the Medieval Age, rumor sometimes supplants the facts, and wisdom is sacrificed for speculation. At times the network turns into a completely uncontrolled town square. There is a constant struggle to bring depth to conversations that are taking place among servers, and intelligent minds can become disillusioned. It is a testimonial to an age of misinformation. In this world of unreality, the academic and social challenge for instructors is to navigate through the "clutter" and accumulate a true body of knowledge.

Though we rearrange our society around technology, we need to make peace with it. This is the concept of embeddedness, or a reality where technology loses its "wow" factor and becomes the paper/pencil/calculator/toaster of our current environment. The basic message is to try to improve education in ways that are important. The way to do this is to turn the focus back on the individual. Education is still about instructors helping students acquire and construct knowledge. Human beings will ultimately become more important in the future as technologies continue to allow us to challenge and extend our communication capabilities. As a foundation, there is a need for limited understanding and desire for technology in education. Instructors and course designers are at the epicenter for deciding what to do that is purposeful with technology in Web-based environments. The ability to find and utilize credible resources on the Web gives the control back to teachers in deciding how we are going to equip students to function in this world. It is an immense responsibility with the swell of resources, new tools, and new capabilities they provide.

In order to overcome these challenges, teachers need to communicate with others who have already made the commitment to new technology. Look for resources, experts, mentors, communities, and staff development or training not only to acquire and use these tools but also for simple generation and exchange of ideas. This process will allow educators to avoid learning alone and encourage them to share ideas, team with peers, and put their new findings up on the Web for greater sharing and potential impact.

Comfort can be taken in the fact nobody is an expert in the technology field for very long. Technology and its capabilities are changing every day. Instructors must realize that they are students and students are teachers, too. Everyone is working in a collaborative learning workspace in most online environments.

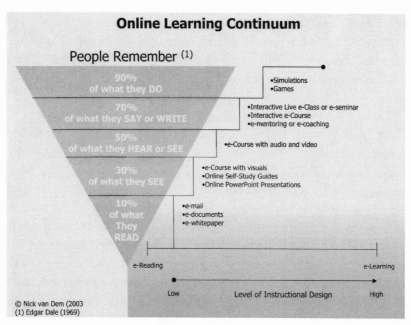

Figure 6.1. *Online Learning Continuum*

Based on the consumer and entertainment industries to which students have grown accustomed, instructors must change from traditional "lecture on chalkboard" methods of yesterday to the online environments of today. New technological tools bring a new and different set of rules and capabilities. Information is organized in a non-linear format with no set method for accessing and using that information. Educators will continue to adjust their instructional strategies to the learning styles of students. Streaming video, audio, cable TV, and online gaming, among others, are what teachers are competing against. Visual instruction is a reaction to the growth of visual media in popular culture. We see this in the amount of choices available (e.g., TV channels, Web sites, and movies). High use of technology and hands-on experiences keep classes enthralled right to the end of the course by integrating as many of the senses as possible, which is more impressionable on the brain. Through using these new technologies, instructors and course designers can make learning interesting, exciting, and fun. Effective use of technology will equal effective teaching.

The future is now. These novel technologies and the Internet have become the scientific tools allowing us to explain hard-to-understand phenomena. The visions and purposeful application of technology instructors, plus motivated students with access to technologies, is the formula for success. If students can hear, see, and try concepts through various technologies, they will experience higher retention and learn faster while maintaining interest in the content area. Instructors need to get students involved in every way. Curriculum does not have to change at all; instead, its presentation and manipulation by the student needs to be reconceptualized. Technology simply adds an additional resource to the course.

ONLINE TEACHING AND LEARNING: THE WINNING COMBINATION

In most classrooms, education methods have remained the same. Traditional methods include instruction such as teachers focusing on students being able to recall facts, concepts, and formulae through lectures and

textbooks. In this method, knowledge is based on how much information the student has been exposed to and the ability to recall this information. However, research tells us that traditional methods of education
do not produce the highest levels of learning. Linn (1986) demonstrates
that "research on learning by cognitive scientists has demonstrated quite
convincingly that students learn by constructing their own understandings based on personal observation and experience, rather than by remembering what others tell them." Knapp and Glenn (1994) suggest
that retention of information is enhanced when students are actively involved in the learning process and can apply this knowledge to new situations: "Students learn, not by listening to information presented by
others, but by actively manipulating and synthesizing information in
such a way that it complements and expands existing understandings."

Technology has a central role to play in creating and sustaining the
conditions for actively manipulating and synthesizing information. A
growing body of research collected over the last decade serves as proof
of the impact of technology in collaborative Web-based environments
on student outcomes.

Our Research Findings

Our most recent focus group of 85 students and 15 alumni explored
and examined program-development recommendations, trends, and
global implications (see table 6.2). In analyzing these data sources from
the past four years across the online master's in educational technology
program, we were able to widen the research sample and increase the
confidence level of results. This was done by identifying and describing several key elements and patterns of learning and growth that are
important to student performance achievement and what students at-
tribute to part of their growth during the program.

To set up an effective online environment, we found the following
elements must be considered:

- Learning model needs to be collaborative and approached as a
  team effort.
- Professors act as guides, mentors, and even co-learners.
- Student opinion and experience is valued by professors and peers.

- Students are challenged to apply new knowledge and share what happened as a result. This challenge changes knowledge into something owned, not memorized.
- Select tools for both synchronous and asynchronous communication.
- Include learning technologies: chat rooms, threaded discussions, video streaming, audio streaming, simulations, and laboratories.
- Decide on activities and projects (a.k.a., what to do where?).
- Make projects and assignments open ended. Interactive set-up includes distributed collaborators, Web-based inquiry, case application, rich media, and public demonstration of learning.
- Determine how work will be evaluated (i.e., peer review and percent of grade given on collaboration) and communicate it to students.
- Determine how you will provide feedback (i.e., emails, privacy, and frequency).
- Set schedule for synchronous meetings. Consider student input.
- Set expectations for asynchronous discussion every day, several times per week.
- Limit Group size (i.e., 20–25 for newsgroups 3–5 for group projects).
- Provide orientation if required (e.g., Tech Camp, tech remediation, and community help).

Unlike a traditional classroom that moves in lockstep to a well-defined syllabus (one that is measured by minutes and hours), learning is sometimes difficult to observe—even by those involved in the collaborative effort. The advantage to a collaborative community is the direct involvement that is required for the acquisition of knowledge. One student observed, "Ideas are out there for all to see and comment on, which lends itself to our examining of what we are doing and learning . . . . We get to see the big picture." There was a shift from an emphasis on the individual learner to an emphasis on a shared community. Rather than being told what to do, they are guided in how to accomplish something that they have decided upon. Giving students choices in layers of communication for synchronous communication (e.g., chat, video-conferencing, instant messaging, and telephone conversations) allows students a greater amount of ownership and confidence when working in collaboration with other students. Their vested interest in the outcome is an important factor when it comes to motivation because the learning is no longer an external manifestation that is held inside a textbook; rather the learning is internal and depends on their decisions of what to include or exclude. As one student reflected, "How rewarding it is to read an article, feel a strong reaction, type this into NG [newsgroup], and read someone else's reaction in a few hours! In a traditional setup, I'd have to wait until next week's class."

It is difficult to be a non-participant without falling back into the traditional mode of learning by rote and explicit isolation of sharing knowledge. "The assignments utilizing technology are not just busywork, but are thought provoking and challenging—much more so than any undergraduate or graduate classes that I've ever had. Always before the learning has been self-contained.... [Now] we rely on cadre members for help, support, information and feedback. That makes a world of difference. The technology involved makes that possible," said B. G. Garnett in October 2001.

Both instructors and students prosper when instructors initiate and facilitate their learning environment with dynamic communication methods that foster and support student-to-student communication and collaboration. Specifically, it 1) aids college faculty in designing courses; 2) guides teacher-education students in integrating educational technology in K–16 courses; and 3) helps instructional trainers in developing Web-based training materials. Our goal is that educators benefit by developing an awareness and knowledge of the potential in online teaching.

An essential piece in the planning for online courses is in thinking about *when* technology is the best tool to accomplish the work involved. The fact is tools may change over time. Things that continually have presence in learning are the learning process, dialogue, idea of apprenticing, culture, shared knowledge or co-creation of knowledge, and an authentic context. The connecting factor of a learning community, we found, is a common goal (i.e., project within the learning group), which is essential for complete success. Tables 6.1 and 6.2, which show the compiled enrollment data and the program participant feedback, were adapted from "A Model for Shaping the Learning Environment

Table 6.1.   Compiled Enrollment Data

Enrollment Yr.	Education	Business	Total Yr.	Drop	Graduated	Percentages
1998	14	10	24	1	20	83.33%
1999	37	25	62	1	58	93.55%
2000	48	26	74	2	67	90.54%
2001	35	28	63	1	59	96.83%
2002	42	31	73	7	64	87.67%
Totals			296	12	268	90.54%

for Effective Web Based Courses: Pepperdine's Online Master's in Educational Technology Program," by Mercedes M. Fisher, Pepperdine University; and Bonita Coleman, Bellflower Christian Schools.

Appropriate application of technologies in the online classroom allows students to create knowledge by giving them opportunities to explore, interact, problem solve, and collaborate, among others. The multi-sensory and interactive capabilities of technologies can enhance the learning of all students regardless of prior experience, exceptionalities, or cultural backgrounds. Instructors are wrestling with finding and implementing appropriate roles for these new technologies in their online courses.

In the next five years, instructors will revolutionize the educational process through the instructional strategies for teaching in Web-based environments explored in the preceding pages. It is analogous to the situation of math teachers, who first resisted the use of calculators but now applaud the benefits that advances in calculator technology bring

Table 6.2   Program Participant Feedback

Benefits and Sustained Results (In order of popular idea and preference from participants)	1. Networking and relationships 2. Mentoring and Leadership 3. Communication 4. Knowledge sharing and management 5. Ethics 6. Diversity education (connecting across barriers)
Global Thinking and World Trends	1. Project based learning; hands on approach 2. Community action; seeing results 3. Transcends barriers and expands walls 4. Education worldwide
Implications	1. Collaboration
Suggestions	2. Establishes partnerships 1. Expand existing courses to include international collaboration

to problem-solving activities. Our hope is that with the new capabilities, technologies afford instructors and course designers will help plan the future rather than let the future drive them. The vision is that online courses will demonstrate access to learning achievement in ways that have not been possible before.

An entirely new and revolutionary educational system is at hand, one that allows instructors to continually have better access for communication with peers, online communities, experts, and information. This availability of quality resources for an instructor is just as important as good surgical materials for a surgeon; however, materials and access alone do not make the difference. It is critical that instructors understand what they are trying to teach, as well as what students are trying to learn.

Technology will transform the way the educational message is delivered. But it is the message, the piece of knowledge, that is most important. Instructors must still spend an equal amount of time and attention on the message that is being delivered, primarily, how it is being delivered. Hence, the primary purpose of these technological tools is in bringing the message and delivery together and making them available on a personal basis.

Take the First Step

The teacher is the vital ingredient that pulls the message, media, and curriculum together. Students will become more committed to learning because they will not be asked the traditional questions and given the same old lectures. Instructors should create and model an image for the use of technology in their courses for learning and the skills they want their students to acquire. As a result, students will be trained on the Web-communication and skill capabilities that are being used in today's industry, making what they learn "real world" applicable. Students will be encouraged to begin collaborating beyond scheduled course times and course members. Most importantly, students will have time to think critically and reflect about problems rather than spending most of their course time finding information. Students turn information into knowledge by giving it meaning. Technologies simply help open their eyes to the world around them.

What is needed is action. That is exactly the purpose of this book—educators taking action, action that responds to the ever-changing needs of today's students. It is vital that these online environments be integrated and utilized for learning in courses. The most positive of all aspects is the transition from passive learner to active learner. In a society where entertainment is such a huge market, technologically supported courses are capable of competing by involving the student in fun and challenging modes of education. The technology's capabilities and resources can transform static, generalized learning into profoundly personal and meaningful interactive experiences that help instructors broaden the reach, and add dimensions to, the learning experience and exploit the incredible energy and emotion bottled up inside their students in ways that are both practical and powerful.

So regardless of your experience—whether you are a novice instructor or a "seasoned" professional—you can use the information, instructional strategies, principles, activities, and processes outlined in this book to make decisions about pedagogical issues and to become a better course designer and facilitator. You can create online courses with the image you want and the impact you need. We wish you success!

Appendix A: Technology Resources

Technology resources simplify the tasks of creating these online courses. New resources are continually being released.

Information Architecture Resources

www.jjg.net/ia/
www-3.ibm.com/ibm/easy/eou_ext.nsf/Publish/570
www.tc.umn.edu/~jveldof/ACRL99/bib.html

Social Network Analysis

semanticstudios.com/publications/semantics/000006.php
www.orgnet.com/sna.html
www.oreillynet.com/pub/a/webservices/2002/06/04/udell.html
stat.gamma.rug.nl/socnet.htm

Etienne Wenger—Stewarding Knowledge

hale.pepperdine.edu/~dlkilbur/fall2002/633/cop_leadership.php

Sample of Curriculum-related Approaches

Harvard Teaching for Understanding and Active Learning Practices for Schools
learnweb.harvard.edu/

4MAT
www.aboutlearning.com/
Project Zero
www.pz.harvard.edu/
Designing for Learning: The Pursuit of Well-Structured Content
www.syllabus.com/article.asp?id=7092
Dimensions in Learning
www.mcrel.org/products/dimensions/whathow.asp
Problem-based Learning
www.ascd.org/readingroom/edlead/9304/stepien.html
Socratic Seminar
socratic.org/www.ncsu.edu/literacyjunction/html/tutorialsocratic.html
Skillful Teacher (Research for Better Teaching)
www.rbteach.com/
Guidelines for Best Practice in Learning Community Assessment
www.iastate.edu/~learncommunity/guidelines.html
Learning Object Repositories
www.edusource.ca/
Learning Suites: Marshall University Web site
www.marshall.edu/it/cit/webct/compare/comparison.html
Georgia Southern University on Synchronous Communication;
www2.gasou.edu/facstaff/jwalker/tutorials/cte.html

Organizations

ASCD Association for Supervision and Curriculum Development
www.ascd.org/
U.S. Department of Education
www.ed.gov/index.jsp
Office of Educational Technology at USDOE
www.ed.gov/Technology/
The National Educational Technology Plan
www.ed.gov/Technology/elearning/index.html
Vocational and Adult Education
www.ed.gov/offices/OVAE/
Cognitive Arts (Roger Schank's company)
www.corporate.cognitivearts.com/exec/corporate/index.cfm

ISTE International Society for Technology in Education
  www.iste.org/
NSTA National Science Teacher Association
  www.nsta.org/
NCTM National Council of Teachers of Mathematics
  www.nctm.org/
NCTE National Council of Teachers of English
  www.ncte.org/
Education resource for state-by-state curriculum links
  edstandards.org/Standards.html
A collection of ideas from notable cognitive science engineers
  www.edge.org/
Technology standards by ISTE
  www.iste.org/standards/
Online article from Grant Wiggins about curriculum
  www.elm.maine.edu/library/pdf/futility.pdf
Index of Professional Distance Education Organizations
  www.uwex.edu/disted/assoc.html

Readings: Project Based Learning

4Teachers - PBL - What is It?
  www.4teachers.org/projectbased/
West Ed.
  pblnet.org
Project-based Learning
  www.bgsu.edu/organizations/ctl/proj.html
Buck's Institute
  www.bie.org
CORD - Leading Change in Education
  www.cord.org/lev2.cfm/65
Project Approach
  www.webproject.org
AutoDesk Foundation
  www3.autodesk.com
Research
  www.edweek.org/ew/1999/29boaler.h18

Multimedia
  www.artmuseum.net/w2vr/timeline/timeline.html
Story
  teachervision.com/lesson-plans/lesson-4727.html

Readings: Constructivism

  www.ilt.columbia.edu/k12/livetext/docs/construct.html
  www.inform.und.edu/UMS+State/UMDProjects/MCTP/
  www.inform.umd.edu/UMS+State/UMDProjects/MDCTP/Essays/
    Strategies.txt
  curriculum.calstatela.edu/faculty/psparks/theorists/501const.htm

Readings: Multiple Intelligences

Howard Gardner
  adulted.about.com/education/adulted/library/weekly/aa061900b.htm
  hale.pepperdine.edu/~jpotter/howard_gardner_multiple_i.htm

Readings: Bloom's Taxonomy

  www.coun.uvic.ca/learn/program/hndouts/bloom.html
  faculty.washington.edu/krumme/guides/bloom.html
Task Wheel
  www.stedwards.edu/cte/resources/bwheel.htm

Readings: SCANS Report

  www.academicinnovations.com/report.html

Readings: Engaged Learning

  www.ncrel.org/sdrs/engaged.htm

Readings: Backward Design

  www.ascd.org/readingroom/books/wiggins98toc.html

Readings: Issues in Technology

Critical Issues
www.ncrel.org/sdrs/areas/te0cont.htm
Ed. Technology
www.ed.gov/Technology/techconf/2000/
Pros/Cons
edtechnot.com
Bibliography
www.ncrel.org/sdrs/areas/techbib.htm
Resource for Writing Learning Objectives
www.e-learingguru.com/articles/art3_4.htm
Assessment
www.ncrel.org/enguage/framewk/efp/align/efpalisu.htm
Design for Learning
www.cast.org/udl
Achievement
ets.org/researchpic/technolog.html
Tech Counts
edweek.com/reports
Standards
www.iste.org/Standards/ncate/basic.html
Tech Learning
techlearning.com/content/reviews/articles/hotlist_resrch.html
Syllabus
www.syllabus.com
Encyclopedia of Educational Technology
coe.sdsu.edu/eet/Admin/TOC/index.htm
World's Largest Online Library
www.questia.com
Communication
www.nettskolen.com/alle/forskning/19/cmcped.html
Teacher Use
nces.ed.gov/pubsearch/pubsinfo.asp?pubid=2000090
New Roles
bogota.soehd.csufresno.edu/devo_ogd/dissertation.pdf
The New Plagiarism
fno.org/may98/cov98may.html

Interactive Online Game

The Reconstructors has students' work as scientists, historians, geographers, and detectives.
reconstructors.rice.edu/
Create a Game
www.stagecast.com
Taxonomy of Computer Games
www.vancouver.wsu.edu/fac/peabody/game-book/Chapter3.html
Game Studies
www.gamestudies.org/0101/juul-gts/
National Board Certification
www.nbpts.org

Tools resource sites

Web development
hotwired.lycos.com/webmonkey/
Web-page goodies
www.bravenet.com
Graphics
graphsearch.com
Planet PDF
www.planetpdf.com
Bibliography
www.noodletools.com/noodlebib/index.html
Web-site tools
landmark-project.com
Web Developer Sites
www.w3.org
www.builder.com
www.webdevelop.com
www.iboost.com
www.wdvl.com
www.bignosedbird.com
Publicizing Your Site
www.addme.com

www.submit-it.com

www.promotionworld.com

Accessible Web Pages: Advice for Educators

www.syllabus.com/article.asp?id=7095

HTML Validators

www.netmechanic.com

www.cast.org/bobby

www2.imagiware.com/RxHTML

validator.w3.org

WebQuest Template

www.kiko.com/wqst

Online Discussion

www.server.com

Web-site tools

trackstar.hprtec.org

Rubric, Quizzes, etc.

www.4teachers.org/tools/index.shtml

Online Journal

www.blogger.com

Online Communities Resources

Yahoo Groups

groups.yahoo.com

MSN Groups

groups.msn.com/home

AT&T Network: Online Communities for Teachers

www.att.com/learningnetwork/teachers/general.html

Global Educators Network

vu.cs.sfu.ca/GEN/welcome/welcome.html

Brainstorms

brainstorms.rheingold.com

CPSquare: The Community of Practice on Communities of Practice

www.cpsquare.com

Tapped In

www.tappedin.org

Comm. Tech Lab, Michigan State University, Professional Growth

commtechlab.msu.edu/sites/letsnet/noframes/bigideas/b9/b9u216
.htm

A Questioning Tool Kit
  emifyes.iserver.net/fromnow/nov97/toolkit.html
TrackStar
  trackstar.hprtec.org
Streaming Video
  www.stager.org/imovie/streaming.htm
Survey Creation
  www.freeonlinesurveys.com
Citing Electronic Sources
  www.cyberbee.com/citing.html
Internet for Beginners – Learn the Net
  learnthenet.com/english/html/24mlists.htm
Additional citation guides
  www.easybib.com/
  www.apastyle.org/elecref.html
  www.mla.org/www_mla_org/style/style_index.asp?mode=section
  www.library.wisc.edu/libraries/Memorial/citing.htm
Internet Public Library
  www.ipl.org/
OneLook Dictionary Search
  www.onelook.com/
Ohio SchoolNet's eCommunity: Glossary
  www.osn.state.oh.us/5_help/default.asp?pg=2
The Librarian's Index to the Internet
  lii.org/
Understanding grammar and structure of the Internet
  www.edrenplanners.com/infolit/
The Technology Source
  ts.mivu.org/
Encyclopedia of Education Technology
  coe.sdsu.edu/eet/Admin/TOC/index.htm
Cognitive and Technology Group at Vanderbilt
  peabody.vanderbilt.edu/ctrs/ltc/Research/jasper_readings.html
Active Learning in the College Classroom
  www.educ.drake.edu/romig/activelng.html
Teaching with the Case Method
  www.indiana.edu/%7Eteaching/handbook_2.html#case

Classroom Assessment Techniques
www.psu.edu/celt/CATs.html

Concept Mapping
www.coun.uvic.ca/learn/program/hndouts/map_ho.html

Collaborative vs. Cooperative Learning
www.lgu.ac.uk/deliberations/collab.learning/panitz2.html

Critical Thinking
www.criticalthinking.org/university/univclass/Defining.html

Teaching by Discussion
www.psu.edu/celt/newsletter/ID_Dec92.html

Learning by Doing
www.chelt.ac.uk/gdn/

The First Day of Class
teaching.berkeley.edu/bgd/firstday.html

Journal Writing and Adult Learning
www.ericfacility.net/ericdigests/ed399413.html

Effective Use of Student Journal Writing
www.indiana.edu/%7Eeric_rec/ieo/digests/d99.html

Writing for Learning, Not Just for Demonstrating Learning
www.ntlf.com/html/lib/bib/writing.htm

Student-Centered Instruction
www2.ncsu.edu/unity/lockers/users/f/felder/public/Papers/Resist.html

Lectures and Approaches to Active Learning
scholar.lib.vt.edu/ejournals/JVME/V21-1/Seeler1.html

Assessment Using the Multiple-choice Format
www.jmu.edu/assessment/mcformat.htm

Problem-based Learning
www.ntlf.com/html/pi/9812/toc.htm

Peer and Self Assessment
www.tedi.uq.edu.au/gi/module_xpt/peer_mod.html

Principles of Good Practice for Assessing Student Learning
www.aahe.org/principl.htm

Motivating Students
teaching.berkeley.edu/bgd/motivate.html

Writing to Learn
ctl.unc.edu/fyc4.html

Quizzes, Tests, and Exams
   teaching.berkeley.edu/bgd/quizzes.html

While effort has been made to ensure that all of the URLs listed in this appendix are valid, we cannot be held responsible for any bad URLs due to sites relocating or going offline.

Appendix B: Tools

These are some tools we use; this list should be used as a guide (not as a finite reference) for your consideration. Online learning is more than a collection of tools. It's about the community and the learning methods we employ. We change and add to this group as new tools become applicable and available.

- Adobe Acrobat Reader. A free software program for viewing and printing all Adobe Portable Document Format (PDF) files on most major operating systems. It will also enable you to view adobe Photoshop album slide shows and electronic cards. www.adobe .com/products/acrobat/readstep2.html
- Adobe GoLive. Allows you to design, manage, and deploy powerful Web sites. Integrates well with other Adobe products such as Photoshop, Acrobat, and Illustrator. www.adobe.com/products/ golive/main.html
- Adobe LiveMotion. Integrates fully with the other Adobe products such as GoLive and Photoshop. It allows the user to create animated interactive Web pages in a variety of formats such as Flash and Quicktime. www.adobe.com/products/livemotion/splash.html
- Adobe Photoshop. A professional image editing software package that produces high quality images for print, the Web, and anywhere else you can think of. www.adobe.com/products/photoshop/main. html
- Blog (journaling software). From the name WebLog, it is a weblog system that allows you to set up a journal online with different categories. www.blogger.com/about.pyra

- Camtasia Software. A software suite made up of five applications that allows you to record, edit, and share videos of activity on your windows screen. www.techsmith.com/products/studio/default.asp
- Cold Fusion. Allows you to build rich Internet applications that integrate with databases, XML, Web services, and Macromedia MX, as well as other programs. It is a productive scripting environment that allows you to create applications such as advanced Web sites and dynamic publishing systems. www.macromedia.com/software/coldfusion/
- Course Management Tools. Such as Blackboard (www .blackboard.com), WebCT, and TopClass are Internet infrastructure software suites that allow teachers to develop and maintain their online courses as well as create communities and host auxiliary services online with their student population.
- Coursebuilder. An extension of Dreamweaver that allows you to develop complete Web-based learning interactions. It has templates for quizzes and assessment items as well as templates for pre-scripted learning interactions. It also has the ability to track the data using a database program such as Lotus LearningSpace or a learning management system. www.macromedia.com/resources/elearning/extensions/dw_ud/coursebuilder
- Dragon Voice. This is speech-recognition software that enables the user to work faster and more efficiently by speaking into his or her computer and having the words appear on the screen. It can be used to create documents including dittos, memos, surveys, and forms. It integrates with the Microsoft Office Suite. Currently it is only available for PCs. www.1stvoice.com/entry.html shop.voice recognition.com/items.asp?CartId=8036008OXE-ACCWARE-BG122&Cc=DRAGON&tpc=
- Email groups (Yahoo). A list of email addresses of people interested in the same topic. Similar to a newsgroup, but instead of having to go somewhere online to read the messages they are delivered straight to your email account.
- Filemaker Pro. Allows you to organize and track people, objects, images, and information. Also allows people to share via an Intranet or a browser the information they have in their workgroup and communicate quickly and effectively. www.filemaker.com/products/fm_home.html

- Final Cut Pro. A professional nonlinear editor that lets you work in SD, HD, Film, offline, and DV formats. www.apple.com/finalcutpro/
- Fireworks. The easiest way to create, optimize, and export interactive graphics in a single Web-centric environment. www.macromedia. com/software/fireworks/
- Flash. A powerful tool for creating rich Internet content. Flash has vector graphics and animation tools as well as video support such as MPEG, AVI, and MOV formats. You can use Flash to create anything from online advertising and electronic learning courses to multimedia content. www.macromedia.com/software/flash/
- Freehand. A program that allows you to design, produce, and publish graphics in a single system. You can use it to create Flash content. www.macromedia.com/software/freehand/
- Freeway 3.5. Designed for Mac OS X and 9 and generates HTML to help users to build Web content without coding that contains graphics and typography components. www.softpress.com
- iCal. A personal calendar system that allows you to organize your time more efficiently and keep track of your appointments and reminders. www.apple.com/ical/
- iDVD. Allows you to create your own DVDs. Works in harmony with the rest of iLife. www.apple.com/idvd/
- iMovie. A digital video application for Mac users that allows you to capture, edit, and export your audio and video footage. It has many stunning effects and is extremely user friendly. It has sophisticated audio and video controls and allows you to send your iMovie to DVD. www.apple.com/imovie/
- Instant Messenger. A place for real-time or synchronous chat. Examples are MSN Messenger, Yahoo Messenger, and AOL Instant Messenger. Users create accounts and usernames that allow others to find them easily and either chat one on one or in chat rooms they create.
- Intranets. A private mini-Internet that is used inside a closed place such as a company, school, university, business, or organization.
- Intraspect. Knowledge-management software that enables people to collaborate in secure online workspaces, using email, Web browser, and desktop applications to share knowledge and resources, and collaborate and work together. www.intraspect.com/ products/

- iPhoto. An all-in-one application for importing, organizing, editing, and sharing your digital photos. www.apple.com/iphoto/
- iTune. A digital music player that works seamlessly with the rest of the iLife suite that can incorporate your music into your iDVD and iMovie creations. www.apple.com/itunes/
- Macromedia Dreamweaver. Allows you to create, build, and manage Web sites and Internet applications in a single environment. www.macromedia.com/software/dreamweaver/
- Microsoft Office. Microsoft's bundle of productivity tools featuring such programs as Word (word processing), Excel (spreadsheets), Access (databases), and Outlook (email and appointments organizer). www.microsoft.com/office
- Microworlds. A Logo-based curriculum-construction kit that allows the student to program a "turtle." It has many applications in all areas of the school curriculum and is excellent at developing problem solving, critical thinking, and creativity in students. www.microworlds.com/
- Net Meeting. Windows real-time collaboration and conferencing client. www.microsoft.com/windows/netmeeting/
- NetObjects Fusion 7. Allows novices through experts to build Web pages easily by using templates and drag and drop features. www.netobjects.com
- Netscape or newsgroup readers. A browser for the Internet, Netscape has a stable newsgroup reader that you can use as part of their communicator package. A newsgroup reader is used to subscribe to different threaded discussion boards that students can participate in asynchronous chats with. The nice thing about the reader is that it keeps all the newsgroup messages in one spot, and you can sort through the messages by sender, date, and even subject to find what you are looking for. www.netscape.com
- Online surveys. Either create your own online surveys using your Web-editing software such as Dreamweaver in the format of a form, or you can use an online service such as www.freeonlinesurveys. com or do a search for a free online survey builder at www .google.com.
- Palm software. Software that you can download or install on your Palm handheld device. www.palm.com/software/

- QuickTime and Realplayer. Allows you to create, play, and stream video and audio over the Internet. www.apple.com/quicktime/products/qt/ and www.real.com/?pv=0&dp=14us
- Shockwave. Enables you to create animation and entertainment. www.shockwave.com
- Swish. A quick and easy way to create Flash animations for your Web site. You can create shapes, text buttons, and graphics animations and apply animated effects at the click of a button. www.swishzone.com
- Tapped In. This is a tool we use for our synchronous chat sessions. It is an online workplace of an international community of educational professionals. Excellent for engaging in professional-development programs and collaboration activities online. www.tappedin.org/
- Timbuktu. "Remote and file transfer" software that is perfect for the mobile worker and telecommuter that needs to connect and communicate with other computers. www.netopia.com/en-us/software/products/tb2/index.html
- XanEdu. Instructor's tool used to compile online readings for students in a packet. It has an ever-growing collection of digitized content, online editing tools, and research applications. You can create your own course pack or let them do it for you. It also has a research engine powered by ProQuest. www.xanedu.com/
- XMetaL 3. Allows developers to create custom tools with which any user can build XML and SGML documents. www.corel.com

Appendix C: Online Tutorials

Helpful tutorials simplify and describe the process for Web-creation tasks for instructors and course designers. New products are continually being released.

Publishing Educational Research

www.aera.net/epubs/

Tutorial Find

The Web's newest tutorials. Allows you to search through all types of categories for a tutorial to suit your needs.

www.tutorialfind.com/tutorials/

Macromedia's tutorial site for their products

www.macromedia.com/elearningcenter/

Microsoft Knowledge Base

support.microsoft.com/default.aspx

Internet 4 Classrooms

Helping teachers use the Internet effectively. Contains an area called Online Practice Modules that gives tutorials for a number of major software titles. There is also a link from there to other tutorials on the Web.

www.internet4classrooms.com/index.htm

WebMonkey

The Web Developer's resource.

hotwired.lycos.com/webmonkey/

Tools for Web Publishing

www.somers.k12.ny.us/intranet/Web_des/tools/extended_
resources.html

Flash

www.echoecho.com/flash.htm
webreference.com/multimedia/flash/

Tech Learning

The resource for education technology leaders.

www.techlearning.com/db_area/archives/WCE/archives/tutorial.
html

Microworlds

www.stager.org/articles/tamagotchi.html
www.southwest.com.au/~jfuller/logotut/menu.htm

While effort has been made to ensure that all of the URLs listed in this appendix are valid, we cannot be held responsible for any bad URLs due to sites relocating or going offline.

Appendix D: Journals

Online journals, indices, and technology news will help get you thinking about future trends in the field and new ideas you might want to try out in your course or workplace.

List of Useful Journals

The following list of journals contains articles relevant to educational computing and should be used as a guide (not as a finite reference) for your review.

British Journal of Educational Technology
Computer-Assisted English Language Learning Journal
Computers & Education: An International Journal
Computers and the Humanities
Computers in Human Behavior
Computers in the Schools
CyberPsychology and Behavior
Education, Communication & Information
Educational Technology
Educational Technology Research and Development
First Monday (peer-reviewed journal on the Internet)
Human Computer Interaction
Information Resources Management Journal
Information Technology in Childhood Education Annual
Interactive Learning Environments
Interactive Multimedia Journal of Computer Enhanced Learning

International Journal of Artificial Intelligence in Education
International Journal of Educational Technology
International Journal of Educational Telecommunications
International Journal of Instructional Media
Journal of Computer Assisted Learning
Journal of Computers in Mathematics and Science Teaching
Journal of Computing in Teacher Education
Journal of Curriculum Studies
Journal of Database Management
Journal of Educational Computing Research
Journal of Educational Media
Journal of Educational MultiMedia & HyperMedia
Journal of Educational Technology Systems
Journal of End User Computing
Journal of Global Information Management
Journal of Information Technology for Teacher Education
Journal of Interactive Learning Research
Journal of Interactive Media in Education
Journal of Interactive Online Learning
Journal of Online Learning and Technology
Journal of Open and Distance Learning
Journal of Research on Computing in Education
Journal of Science Education and Technology
Journal of Special Education Technology
Journal of Technology and Teacher Education
Journal of Technology Education
Logo Exchange
Networks: Online Journal for Teacher Research
Office of Learning Technologies; Online Journal Resources
Simulation and Gaming
Simulation Games for Learning
The Quarterly Review of Distance Education

Indices

Education Index
Current Index of Journals in Education CIJE
Educational Resources Information Center database ERIC

Other Educational Periodicals

Subject-specific and population-specific (e.g., gifted or special needs) educational journals offer regular articles on the use of technology in education. For example, *The Mathematics Teacher*, the *Journal of Staff Development* and the *Music Educators Journal* have published special issues integrating technology.

Tech News

CNET's news.com
  news.com.com/
CNN - Technology: Computing
  www.cnn.com/TECH/
The Industry Standard: MEDIA GROK
  www.thestandard.com/news/features/
Good Morning Silicon Valley (*San Jose Mercury*)
  www.bayarea.com/mld/mercurynews/
MacInTouch Home Page
  www.macintouch.com/
The New York Times: Technology
  www.nytimes.com/
Slashdot
  slashdot.org/
Wired Magazine
  www.wired.com/wired/current.html
Technology & Learning Magazine
  www.techlearning.com
ZDNNews: Page One
  zdnet.com.com/

Appendix E: Instructor's Web Site

In the following pages you will see samples of how I have used the theories discussed in this book to organize and fill with content my course Web site. The information I have provided in these samples includes but is not limited to:

- student guidelines and helpful hints
- activities
- additional resources

I hope by providing you with these visual layouts I have given you a clear vision of where to begin your own design.

gsep.pepperdine.edu/~mmfisher/main/discussions.html
gsep.pepperdine.edu/~mmfisher/main/resources.html
gsep.pepperdine.edu/~mmfisher/main/videos.html
gsep.pepperdine.edu/~mmfisher/main/upcoming.html
gsep.pepperdine.edu/~mmfisher/664/664digital.html
gsep.pepperdine.edu/~mmfisher/664/664objectives.html
gsep.pepperdine.edu/~mmfisher/664/664grppro1.htm
gsep.pepperdine.edu/~mmfisher/main/sitemap.html

Appendix F: Real-time Chat Activity

1. Break class off into groups for 10–12 minutes to discuss chapters of assigned readings.
2. Come back into one group for a quick share (chapters of case book).
3. The instructor should direct students off to a Web site she projected on two other cases.
4. Students e-journal for 5–7 minutes and then come together again to discuss as a group the two cases.
5. After class have students e-journal on the change in approach and ask if the group dialogue changed the way the group listened to one another?

alignment. Arrangement or positioning of type elements with respect to left and right margins (flush left, flush right, or justified).

alternate assessment. Any type of assessment where students create a response to a question or task. (In traditional assessments, students choose a response from a given list, such as multiple choice, true/false, or matching.)

anchored collaboration. A situation where the learners have instructor–provided, structured collaboration opportunities around a main topic or issue. Planned collaboration on structured problems or questions.

animation. The capability of presentation and software to create illusions of movement.

artifact. Typically is something created by humans, usually for a practical purpose, or an object remaining from a particular period. In the context of the Pepperdine model an artifact is documentation, of any form, of the process of one's learning over the course of the program. An artifact helps in producing understanding through interpretation

asynchronous. When using the computer for transmission of conversation, there is no timing requirement. This type of discussion or transmittal of feedback would occur when using email or a posting environment such as threaded discussions.

authentic. Something worthy of acceptance or belief as conforming to or based on fact, as in authentic data or authentic documentation.

backward design. A method of curriculum design wherein planning teachers begin their unit design with their stated standards and end up with classroom activities. The traditional phrase "begin with the end in mind" is used to describe this method of curriculum design.

bandwidth. The amount of network capacity available to carry information and files over the network to your desktop.

blended learning. Used to describe the combination of two specific forms of interaction, online and face to face, when they are used to enhance a learning experience.

browsers. Software programs that interpret the HTML and present the sought-after Web page, allowing users to surf and explore the Internet.

CD/ROM (compact disc, read-only memory). A small storage device that cannot be erased or written over.

chat. Allows two or more users with client software to join, via the Internet, a synchronous, live, online typed discussion usually with participants separated by distance. The server broadcasts all messages to everyone participating in the discussion.

chunking. The theory that all information should be presented in small digestible units, otherwise known as "chunks." Research has shown that presenting information in small units increases the learner's chance of understanding and remembering content.

cognitive. An act or process of knowing something. This knowing includes both awareness and judgment.

collaboration. The act of working jointly with others in an intellectual endeavor.

collaborative. Characterized by interdependency among students. Interdependence is characterized by the necessity to share information, meanings, conceptions, and conclusions; a division of labor wherein roles of team members complement one another on a joint endeavor and the end product requires pooling of different roles; and the need for joint thinking in explicit terms that can be examined, changed, and elaborated on by peers.

communities of practice. A group of people who share similar goals, and in their attempt to reach these goals, they work with the same tools and express themselves to one another in a common language. In this example of a community of practice the common language is spoken through the online environment.

compressed video. Video signals that are downsized to travel along a smaller carrier.

compression. A strategy used to reduce the size of a file without losing any of its original information. Content is completely recovered by reversing the process.

constructionism. An epistemological framework concerned with the building of things, both in the sense of building understanding and building artifacts. In the context of learning theory, constructionism holds that people, and more specifically, children, learn best when they are in the active role of the designer and constructor of information. Cognitive constructionism focuses on the individual learner. Social constructivism emphasizes learning happening within the situation of dialogue and social interaction.

constructionist. Someone who teaches under the pedagogy that students construct their learning in a social way and that the learning that is occurring is a result of something meaningful to the student.

constructivism. A learning theory that supports the idea that learning is an active process in which learners construct new ideas or concepts based upon their current and/or past knowledge.

constructivist. Student-centered instruction characterized by inquiry–driven, authentic problem-solving scenarios where students collaboratively negotiate meaning through creative and critical exploration of alternatives that facilitate the social construction of knowledge.

cyberspace. A term used for the conceptual space in which words and humans interact using computer-mediated communication over networks.

dialogue. An exchange of ideas and opinions that leads to shared meaning.

digital portfolio. The use of the World Wide Web to create a complete picture of one's academic or professional skills and accomplishments by the creation of a Web site that reflects projects, videos, journals, personal information, etc.

distributed collaborators. People who are working together on an idea or project from a distance.

distributed learning. An alternate instructional paradigm incorporating the use of Internet technologies to break the traditional method of teaching by telling. Messages, experiences, and interpersonal interaction flow across networks and form synchronous, virtual learning communities.

drag and drop. A technique to move a file between directories in a graphical user interface. The user can drag a file by clicking its icon with the left-hand mouse button pushed down and moving the mouse pointer. The file is dragged along, and when the user lets go of the file pointer, the icon is dropped.

e-learning. Learning that occurs electronically over the Internet in some fashion.

electronic whiteboard. An application that enables two or more users to share a Web-based "chalkboard" device.

emote. To express emotion using written symbols.

enduring understandings. Concepts created by the instruction in the backward-design process that reflect what knowledge, concepts, or "big ideas" the learner is to walk away from the course comprehending.

expert. A person who is highly skilled and knowledgeable in a given topic.

formative assessment. A diagnostic use of assessment tools to provide feedback to teachers and students over the course of instruction.

frames. Contain multiple HTML pages. Frames enable regions of a page to remain stationary while other regions of a page change (e.g., navigation links).

Gestalt learning. A theory based on analysis of the unified whole, suggesting that the understanding of the entire process is better then the study of the individual parts or sequences of the whole.

hypertext markup language (HTML). The code used to create a homepage; it is used to access documents over the Web.

instructional strategy. An overview of how information will be presented and how students and teachers will interact in an educational program.

instructional technology. The research in and application of strategies and techniques derived from behavioral, cognitive, and constructivist theories to the solution of instructional learning or performance problems.

interdependence. Members of a group must need one another and have a stake in each person's understanding and success. For example, each person has a piece of a map. The group members must each use their own piece of the map for the group to reach their destination.

Internet. A worldwide network of computer networks that are connected to one another using similar protocols. The Internet allows the exchange of files and allows remote connection of a computer client to a server.

KWL. An instructional technique wherein instructors stimulate a students' prior knowledge by asking what they already Know; collaborating with students, as a whole class or within small groups, to set specify what they Want to learn; and after this activity students discuss what they have Learned. With this technique students are able to apply higher-order thinking strategies that help them construct meaning from what they read and help them monitor their progress toward their goals.

learner packet. Hard copy of course materials such as readings, guidelines, assignments, support, resources, etc.

learning environment. On-site or online "place" comprised of an instructor and students.

legibility. Refers to how something looks, how easy it is to recognize short bursts of text, such as titles, buttons, symbols, icons, etc. In print and on screen, sans serif typefaces are more legible.

lifelong learning. A concept, with collaboration and cooperation at its roots, that seeks to build an ongoing relationship between students of all ages and backgrounds to educational institutions.

links. Hypertext connections between Web pages or sections of the current Web page.

listserv. Email mailing list software for sending out messages to a group of subscribers who have a shared interest in a topic. Once a message is sent to the listserv, copies are immediately sent to everyone on the list. Listservs are commonly used to host Internet discussion groups.

metacognitive. The ability to guide one's own comprehension by analyzing how one is learning.

mindful. To be aware. A mindful learner is present in the teachable moment and open to and aware of different kinds of educational theories and practices.

mirror Web site. A Web site that displays corresponding material in exactly the same way on a different file server.

modem. An electronic device that links your computer through a telephone line to the online world by converting the digital information to analog.

multimedia. An approach to learning, using, involving, or encompassing several forms of media.

multi-user object-oriented (MOO) environment. A text-based computer-mediated communication environment that logs discussions and is bounded by time but not place.

netiquette. The generally accepted social skills, understanding, and rules of network etiquette. For example: Be polite and do not insult others.

network. A group of computers connected electronically that allows users to exchange information.

newsgroups. Posts to threads of discussion on topics related to a course of study that can be seen by all who subscribe to that particular newsgroup.

online. Taking place over the Internet, sharing a "workspace" accessed by the World Wide Web. Active and prepared for operation.

open-ended assignments. Tasks that are permitted to or are designed to permit spontaneous and unguided responses.

optimal. Ideal—facilitating a learning environment that is characterized by inquiry-based, creative, and critical thinking, while anticipating and counteracting all contingencies that would impede this from taking place.

pedagogical. Practices relating to or befitting a teacher or education.

pixels. The tiny dots of light (picture elements) that form characters and objects on a computer monitor. The clarity of the monitor is determined by the pixel resolution (the density of pixels).

posting. Writing a reply to a message in a threaded discussion.

project-based learning. An approach to instruction that makes a move away from traditional classroom practices of short, isolated, teacher-centered lessons and instead emphasizes learning activities that are long-term, interdisciplinary, student centered, and integrated with real-world issues and practices.

readability. Refers to how something reads; the format and content are easy to read and understand.

reification. Refers to the process of giving form to experience by producing.

role plays. Used to introduce necessary alternative perspectives into a dialogue.

sans serif. Typeface characters designed without serifs (small strokes on the ends of the main character stems).

schema. A mental structure by which the individual organizes his or her perceptions of the environment.

serif fine. Cross strokes or flares at the end of a letter's main stems.

sharable-content objects. Also known as learning objects. Generally understood to be digital entities deliverable over the Internet, meaning that any number of people can access and use them simultaneously.

simulation tool. A tool that provides an abstraction or simplification of some real-life situation or process.

situated learning. A comprehensive understanding involving the whole person.

streaming media. A strategy of building video, audio, and other multimedia available in real time with no download wait over the Internet or Intranet. Students will need players to view, which are downloadable from the Web for free in most cases.

summative assessment. A diagnostic use of assessment to provide feedback to teachers and students after a period of instruction. This requires making a judgment about the learning that has occurred (e.g., grading a test or paper).

synchronous. When using the computer for transmission of conversation, there is a timing requirement. Conversations take place in real time; interaction among participants is simultaneous. This type of discussion or transmittal of feedback would occur when using instant messaging or another form of real-time chat.

template. An image that serves as background or framework for content to be placed in for online courses. Templates add consistency and continuity. Many templates can be easily created; course software also provides many pre-designed templates that can also be customized.

threaded discussion. Asynchronous discussion where a series of messages and/or comments to the original post are listed below. A discussion may feature multiple threads.

traditional classroom. A classroom consisting of desks, books, chalkboards, and other classroom paraphernalia associated with schools. Communities today are formed around issues of identity, shared values, as well as shared interests and are not necessarily place based (Palloff, 1998). Following this line of thought, Dede (1998) expounded on the power of immersion in a virtual environment. He stated that one's actions and words in such a surreal setting have novel consequences that create a pull and intrigue with the overall experience. This type of discovery process power to shape one's environment, to assume someone else's identity in a world that is being created by those immersed in it, Cherny (1999) defines a speech community as a community with shared rules for speaking and interpretations of speech performance. Specialized language helps to unify the members within the community as well as exclude others. Mutual accountability consists of a code of behavior that is expected to be upheld.

typeface. A specific type design, such as Times Roman, Verdana, New Century Schoolbook, Trebuchet, or Chicago. Some people use the terms *typeface* and *font* interchangeably.

Uniform Resource Locator (URL). A standard way to address any resource on the Internet or on an Intranet. The address of a homepage on the World Wide Web.

video clip. A section of videotape.

video conferencing. A teleconference involving a television-type picture as well as voice transmission. The video image may be freeze-frame or full motion video.

virtual. The adjective *virtual* describes things that feel like reality but lack physical substance. A virtual object, for instance, may be one that has no real-life equivalent; however, the persuasiveness of its representation allows us to respond to it as if it were real (Laurel, 1993). The difference between equipment-based virtual reality, which is full of images and sounds, and its counterpart (text based), is that the participants or users are immersed in words rather than visual images. One common thread in equipment-based and text-based virtual reality is that the virtual world can be whatever the designer makes of it (Walker, 1990). Chat or synchronous discourse or conversation is occurring simultaneously between users.

virtual lab. A highly realistic lab that gives the impression of being inside a three-dimensional space.

Web forms. Web forms consist of a number of elements such as text fields for people to type information into, checkboxes, radio buttons, pull-down menus for making choices, and submit and reset buttons. Lets you collect information from users. Common uses for forms include surveys, order forms, and search interfaces.

Bibliography

Allen, R. 1998. The Web: Interactive and multimedia education. *Computer Networks and ISDN Systems* 30: 1717–27.

Arbaugh, J. B. 2001. How instructor immediacy behaviors affect student satisfaction and learning in Web-based courses. *Business Communication Quarterly* 64: 42–54.

Arias, Ernesto G. 1999. Beyond access: Informed participation and empowerment. In *Proceedings of the Computer Support for Collaborative Learning (CSCL) 1999 Conference*, edited by C. Hoadley and J. Roschelle. Mahwah, N. J.: Lawrence Erlbaum Associates.

Bannan-Ritland, B., N. Dabbagh, and K. Murphy. 2000. Learning object systems as constructivist learning environments: Related assumptions, theories, and applications. In *The instructional use of learning objects: Online version*, edited by D. A. Wiley. At reusability.org/read/chapters/bannan-ritland.doc (accessed October 2002).

Batson, A. D. 1981. Questioning: A reading/thinking foundation for the gifted. Paper presented at the Annual Meeting of the Southwest Regional Conference of the International Reading Association, San Antonio, Texas, January 1981. ERIC Document Reproduction Service No. ED 201 999.

Beer, V. 2000. *The Web learning fieldbook: Using the World Wide Web to build workplace learning environments*. San Francisco: Jossey-Bass Pfeiffer.

Bennett, J. 2000. Hospitality and collegial community: An essay. *Innovative Higher Education* 25, no. 2: 85–96.

Bennett, S., and D. Marsh. 2002. Are we expecting online tutors to run before they can walk? *Innovations in Education and Teaching International* 39, no. 1: 14–20.

Bills, Conrad G. 1997. Effects of structure and interactivity on Internet-based instruction. Paper presented at the Interservice/Industry Training, Simulation, and Education Conference, Orlando, Fla.

Bloom, B. ed. 1967. Cognitive domain. Handbook 1 in *Taxonomy of educational objectives*. New York: Longmans, Green.

Bloom, B. S. 1984. The two sigma problem: The search for methods of group instruction as effective as one-on-one tutoring. *Educational Researcher* 13 (June–July): 4–16.

Bohm, D. 1996. *On dialogue*. New York: Routledge.

Bonk, C. J. 2002. *Online training in an online world*. Bloomington, Ind.: Courseshare.com.

Bostrom, R. 1995. The importance of facilitator role behaviors: Implications for training facilitators to use GSS. *Journal of Teaching International Business* 7, no. 4: 7–30.

Bouas, K., and H. Arrow. 1996. The development of group identity in computer and face-to-face groups with membership change. *Computer-Supported Cooperative Work* 4, no. 2–3: 153–78.

Bourdeau, J., and A. Bates. 1997. Instructional design for distance learning. In *Instructional design: International perspectives*. Vol. 2. *Solving instructional design problems*, edited by S. Dijkstra, M. N. See, F. Scott, and R. A. Tennyson. Mahwah, N. J.: Lawrence Erlbaum Associates.

Brogan, Pat. 1999. *Using the Web for interactive teaching and learning, the imperative for the new millennium*. San Francisco: Macromedia.

Brown, John Seely. 1986. A personal perspective on collaborative tools. Computer Supported Work Conference, Austin, Texas, December 1986.

Bruner, J. 1966. *Toward a theory of instruction*. Cambridge, Mass.: Harvard University Press.

Burmark, Lynell. 2002. *Virtual literacy: Learn to see, see to learn*. Alexandria, Va.: Association for Supervision and Curriuculum Development.

Cherny, L. 1999. Conversation and community: Chat in a virtual world. Stanford, Calif.: Center for the Study of Language and Information.

Clark, Richard. 1983. *Review of Educational Research* 53, no. 4 (Winter): 445–59.

Corey, S. R. 1989. *The seven habits of highly effective people*. New York: Simon and Schuster.

Dede, C. 1998. Learning about teaching and vice versa. Paper presented at Conference of Society for Information Technology in Education. Washington, D.C.

Denzin, N. 1995. *The research act: A theoretical introduction to sociological methods*. Chicago: Aldine.

Diaz, D. P. 2002. Delivering Web-based multimedia using CD/Web hybrids. At ts.mivu.org/default.asp?show=article&id=963 (accessed February 2002).

Dillenbourg, Pierre. 1996. Some technical implications of distributed cognition on the source. *Journal of Artificial Intelligence in Education* 7, no. 2: 161–79.

———, ed. 1999. Collaborative learning: Cognitive and computational approaches. *Advances in Learning and Instruction Series*, January 1, 1999.

DiPetta, T. 1998. Community on-line: New professional environments for higher education. *New Directions for Teaching and Learning* 76: 53–66.

Dixon, Nancy M. 2001. *Perspectives on dialogue making talk developmental for individuals and organizations*. Greensboro, N. C.: Center For Creative Leadership.

Dodge, Bernie. 1998. Introduction to WebQuests. Presented at the National Educational Computing Conference, San Diego, June 22–24, 1998.

Draves, W. 2002. LERN information that works. At www.lern.org (accessed November 2002).

Educational Testing Service/College Board. 1992. 1991 Advanced placement United States history free-response scoring guide and sample student answers. Princeton, N.J.: Educational Testing Service/College Board.

Engelbart, D. C. 1995. Toward augmenting the human intellect and boosting our collective I.Q. *Communications of the ACM* 38, no. 8: 30–33.

Ewall, P. 1994. Restoring our links with society: the neglected art of collective responsibility. *Metropolitan Universities: An International Forum* 5, no. 1: 79–87.

Fisher, M. M. 1998–99. Using Lotus learning space for staff development in public schools. *Journal of Interactive Learning Research* 9, no. 3–4.

———. 1999. Lotus learning space: A WWW strategy for growth. *International Journal of Educational Telecommunications* 5, no. 4.

———. 2000. Implementation considerations for instructional design of Web-based learning environments. In *Instructional and cognitive impacts of Web-based education*, edited by B. Abbey. Hershey, Pa.: Idea Group Publications.

———. 2001–02a. Computer skills of initial teacher education students. *Journal of Information Technology for Teacher Education* 9, no. 1.

———. 2001–02b. Design guidelines for optimum teaching and learning on the Web. *Journal of Educational Technology Systems* 29, no. 2.

Fisher, M. M., and B. C. Coleman. 2001–02. Collaborative online learning in virtual discussions. *Journal of Educational Technology Systems* 30, no. 1.

———. 2002. Creating dynamic learning environments using Web-based delivery. ICCE 2002 International Conference on Computers in Education, Auckland, New Zealand, December 3–6, 2002. Proceedings published by IEEE Computer Society Press.

Fisher, M. M., B. C. Coleman, and P. R. Sparks. In press. Designing collaborative learning in Web-based environments. In Section 2.5.13, Collaboration of Web-based learning framework, of *Web-based learning*, edited by B. H. Khan. Englewood Cliffs, N. J.: Educational Technology Publications.

Fisher, M. M., and Karen Smith-Gratto. 1999. An aid to curriculum and computer integration: Prototypes for teachers. *The Journal of Computers in the Schools* 15, no. 2.

Forman, E., N. Minick, and C. Stone. 1987. *Contexts for learning: Sociological dynamics in children's development*. New York: Oxford University Press.

Fraser, A. B. 1999. Colleges should tap the pedagogical potential of the World Wide Web. *Chronicle of Higher Education*, August 1999, B8.

Gabelnick, F., J. MacGregor, R. Matthews, and B. Smith. 1990. Learning community models. *New Directions for Teaching and Learning* 41: 19–31.

Galagan, Patricia A. 2002. Getting started with e-learning. *Training and Development*, May 2002.

Gallini, J. 2001. A framework for the design of research in technology-mediated learning environments: a sociocultural perspective. *Educational Technology* 41, no. 2: 15–21.

Gamas, W., and C. Nordquist. 1998. Expanding learning opportunities through on-line technology. *NASSP Bulletin* 81, no. 592: 16–22.

Geertz, C. 1973. *The interpretation of cultures*. New York: Basic Books.

Gibbons, A. S., J. Nelson, and R. Richards. 2000. The nature and origin of instructional objects. In *The instructional use of learning objects: Online version*, edited by D. A. Wiley. At reusability.org/read/chapters/gibbons.doc (accessed October 2003).

Glaser, G., and A. Strauss. 1967. *The discovery of grounded theory: Strategies for qualitative research*. Chicago: Aldine.

Green, M. 1978. *Landscapes of learning*. New York: Teachers College Press.

Greeno, J. G. 1997. On claims that answer the wrong questions. *Educational Researcher* 26, no. 1: 5–17.

Gunawardena, C. N. 1991. Collaborative learning and group dynamics in computer-mediated communication networks. In *Research Monograph No. 9 of the Second American Symposium on Research in Distance Education*. University Park: Pennsylvania State University, American Center for the Study of Distance Education, 14–24.

———. 1995. Social presence theory and implications for interaction and collaborative learning in computer conferences. *International Journal of Educational Telecommunications* 1: 147–66.

Guyton, E., and F. Hidalgo. 1995. Characteristics, responsibilities, and qualities of urban school mentors. *Education and Urban Society* 28, no. 1: 40–47.

Guzdial, M., and F. Weingarten, eds. 1995. *Setting a computer science research agenda for educational technology.* Washington, D.C.: Computing Research Association. At www.cc.gatech.edu/gvu/people/faculty/mark. guzdial/EDTECH.pdf.

———. 1996. *Setting a computer science research agenda for educational technology.* Washington, D.C.: Computing Research Association.

———. 1997. *Setting a computer science research agenda for educational technology.* Washington, D.C.: Computing Research Association.

Haavind, S. 2001. *Facilitating online learning: Effective strategies for moderators.* The Concord Consortium. Madison, Wisc.: Atwood Publishing.

Hallinger, P. 1996. Nourishing the spirit: The role of ritual in building communities of learners. *Journal of Staff Development* 17, no. 1: 22–26.

Hannafin, M. J., and S. Hooper. 1989. An integrated framework for CBI screen design and layout. *Computers in human behavior* 5: 155–65.

Hermann, F. 1998. Building on-line communities of practice: An example and implications. *Educational Technology* 38, no. 1: 16–23.

hooks, bell. Women's voices: Quotations by women. At womenhistory. about.com/library/qublquhook.htm (accessed October 2002).

Horgan, B. 1998. Transforming higher education using information technology: First steps. White paper. Microsoft in Education.

Horton, William. 2000. *Designing Web-based training.* New York: John Wiley and Sons.

Howell, D. 2001. Elements of effective e-learning: Three design methods to minimize side effects of online courses. *College Teaching* 49: 87–90.

Husen, T. 1979. General theories in education: A twenty-five-year perspective. *International Review of Education* 25: 325–45.

IRL perspective and principles of learning: Challenging fundamental assumptions. 2003. Pamphlet. Menlo Park, Calif.: Institute for Research on Learning.

Jackson, Steven F. 2001. Online distance education and undergraduate student retention and recruitment. At booboo.webct.com/2001/paper/jackson.pdf (accessed September 2003).

Junk, V., and L. Fox. 1998. Making the most of home pages, e-mail, the Internet and presentation graphics. *T.H.E. Journal* 26, no. 1. At www.the journal.com/magazine/vault/A1998.cfm (accessed July 2001).

Killion, J., and L. Simmons. 1992. The Zen of facilitation. *Journal of Staff Development* 13, no. 3: 2–5.

Klemm, William R. 2002. Extending the pedagogy of threaded-topic discussions. *The Technology Source.* September–October.

Knapp, C. 1994. Progressivism never died, it just moved outside: What experimental educators learn from the past? *Journal of Experimental Education* 17, no. 2: 8–12.

Koffka, K. 1935. *Principles of Gestalt psychology*. 5th ed. London: Kegan Paul.

Kohler, W. 1947. *Gestalt psychology: An introduction to new concepts in modern psychology*. New York: Liveright Publishing.

Kohn, Alfie. 2002. Education's rotten apples. *Education Week*, September 18, 2002. At www.alfiekohn.org/teaching/edweek/rotten.htm.

Krathwohl, D. R., B. S. Bloom, and B. B. Masia. 1964. Affective domain. Handbook 2 in *Taxonomy of educational objectives*. New York: David McKay.

Kuhn, T. 1996. *The structure of scientific revolutions*. Chicago: University of Chicago Press.

Kulik, C. L., and J. A. Kulik. 1986a. Mastery testing and student learning: A meta-analysis. *Journal of Educational Technology Systems* 15, no. 3: 325–45.

——. 1986b. Effectiveness of computer-based education in colleges. *Association of Computer-Based Educational Data Systems Journal* 19, no. 2–3: 81–108.

Kulik, C. L., J. A. Kulik, and R. L. Bangert-Drowns. 1990. Effectiveness of master learning programs: A meta-analysis. *Review of Educational Research* 60, no. 2: 265–99.

Lally, V., and E. Barrett. 1999. Building a learning community on-line: Towards socio-academic interaction. *Research Papers in Education: Policy and Practice* 14: 147–63.

Langer, Ellen J. 1997. *The power of mindful learning*. Cambridge, Mass.: Perseus Books.

Laurel, B. 1993. Computers as theatre. Reading, Mass.: Addison-Wesley.

Lave, J., and E. Wenger. 1991. *Situated learning: Legitimate peripheral participation*. Cambridge: Cambridge University Press.

Leland, K. K. 2003. Can you KaMOO? Ethnography of a virtual learning community. Ph.D. diss., Pepperdine University.

Liaw, S., and H. Huang. 2000. Enhancing interactivity in Web-based instruction: A review of the literature. *Educational Technology* 40, no. 3: 41–45.

Lieberman, A., and M. Grolnick. 1996. Networks of reform in American education. *Teachers College Record* 98, no. 1: 7–45.

Linn, M. C. 1986. Education and the challenge of technology. Paper presented at the Conference on Technology and Teacher Education. Monterrey, California. August 5–8, 1986.

Marzano, Robert J., Debra J. Pickering, and Jay McTighe. 1994. *Assessing student outcomes: Performance assessment using the dimensions of learning model.* n.p.: Association for Supervision and Curriculum Development.

Matthews, R. 1997. Guidelines for good practice: Technology mediated instruction. Paper presented at the Academic Senate for California Community Colleges, Sacramento, Calif., 1997.

McCown, R. R., and M. P. Driscoll. 1995. Using collaborative writing and problem-based learning in the college classroom. Computer Supported Collaborative Learning conference. Bloomington, Indiana.

McKenzie, G. R. 1972. Some effects of frequent quizzes on inferential thinking. *American Educational Research Journal* 9, no. 2: 231–40.

Mehrabian, A. 1971. *Silent messages.* Belmont, Calif.: Wadsworth Publishing.

Moore, P., and C. Fitz. 1993. Gestalt theory and instructional design. *Journal of Technology Writing and Communication* 23, no. 2: 137–57.

Muilenburg, L. and Z. L. Berge. A framework for designing questions for online learning. At emoderators.com/moderators/muilenburg.html (accessed January 2002).

Myers, S. A., M. Zhong, and S. Guan. 1998. Instructor immediacy in the chinese college classroom. *Communication Studies* 49, no. 3: 240–53.

Nielsen, Jakob. 2000. Eyetracking. Study of Web readers. At www.useit.com/alertbox/20000514.html (accessed October 2002).

Norman, D. A. 1993. *Things that make us smart.* Reading, Mass.: Addison-Wesley Publishing.

OMET enrollment and graduation report. Data source Eztrieve (SIS). July 17, 2002.

Online master of arts in educational technology. Proposal submitted to the WASC committee on off-campus and substantive change by the Graduate School of Education and Psychology, Pepperdine University. May 7, 1998.

Orrill, C. H. 2000. Learning objects to support inquiry-based online learning. In *The instructional use of learning objects: Online version,* edited by D. A. Wiley. At reusability.org/read/chapters/orrill.doc (accessed October 2002).

Osterman, K. 2000. Students' need for belonging to the school community. *Review of Educational Research* 70: 323–67.

Palloff, R., and K. Pratt. 1999. *Building learning communities in cyberspace: Effective strategies.* San Francisco: Jossey Bass.

———. 2001. *Lessons from the cyberspace classroom: The realities of online teaching.* San Francisco: Jossey Bass.

Patterson, M. 2002. Online etiquette. *Business Mexico* 11–12: 69.

Peterson, R., and M. Eeds. 1990. *Grand conversations: Literature groups in action*. New York: Scholastic.

Playko, M. 1990. What it means to be mentored. *NASSP Bulletin* 74, no. 526: 29–32.

Polin, L. G. 1999. Educational technology graduate scenarios: Leading Pepperdine's online learning communities. Unpublished document.

Poole, D. M. 2000. Student participation in a discussion-oriented online course: A case study. *Journal of Research on Computing in Education* 33, no. 2: 162–77.

Postmes, T., R. Spears, and M. Lea. 1998. Breaching or building social boundaries? SIDE-effects of computer-mediated communication. *Communication Research* 25: 698–715.

———. 2000. The formation of group norms in computer-mediated communication. *Human Communication Research* 26: 341–71.

Putney, LeAnn G., and Joan Wink. 2002. *A vision of Vygotsky*. Boston: Allyn and Bacon.

Rhodes, C. 1998. Multiple perceptions and perspectives: Faculty/student responses to distance learning. *Technology and Teacher Education Annual* 10: 1089–92.

Richards, Tyde. Shareable content object reference model. At www.adlnet.org/ADLDOCS/Documents/SCORM_1.2_Overview.pdf (accessed October 2002).

Rosenberg, S. 1998. Sad and lonely in cyberspace? *Salon Magazine* 7. At dir.salon.com/21st/rose/1998/09/03straight.htm.

Sachs, P. 1995 Transforming work: Collaboration, learning, and design. *Communications of the ACM* (Special Issue on Representations of Work) 38, no. 9: 36–44.

Salomon, G. 1991. Partners in cognition: Extending human intelligence. *Educational Researcher* (April 1991: 2–10).

———. 1998. Novel constructivist learning environments and novel technologies. *Research Dialogue in Learning and Instruction* 1, no. 1: 3–12.

Salomon, G., and T. Almog. 1998. Educational psychology and technology. *Teachers College Record* 100, no. 1: 222–41.

Scherly, D., L. Roux, and P. Dillenbourg. 2000. Evaluation of hypertext in an activity learning environment. *Journal of Computer Assisted Learning* 16, no. 2: 125–36.

Schiever, S. W. 1991. *A comprehension approach to teaching and thinking*. Boston: Allyn and Bacon.

Schrage, M. 1995. *No more teams: Mastering the dynamics of creative collaboration*. New York: Doubleday.

Sergiovanni, T. 1993. *Building community in schools*. San Francisco: Jossey-Bass.

Shale, D. 1990. Toward a reconceptualization of distance education. In *Contemporary issues in American distance education*, edited by I. M. Moore. New York: Pergarnon.

Shephard, L. 1989. Assessing students' performance. At www.colorado.edu/geography/virtdept/library/activeped/html/section3_1.html (accessed October 2002).

Shotsberger, P. 2000. The human touch: Synchronous communication in Web-based learning. *Educational Technology* 40, no. 1: 53–56.

Smith, John D. Table adapted from E. Wenger. Communities of Practice: Stewarding Knowledge. At groups.yahoo.com/group/com-prac/message/1559 (accessed September 2003).

Smith-Gratto, K., and M. M. Fisher. 1999. Gestalt theory: A foundation for instructional screen design. *Journal of Educational Technology Systems* 27, no. 4.

Song, James Kow Kim. 1998. Using the World Wide Web in education and training. Conference IT in Education and Training. Ho Chi Minh City, Vietnam, January 15–16, 1998.

Spady, William. 1994a. Choosing outcomes of significance. *Educational Leadership* 51, no. 6 (March 1994): 18–22.

———. 1994b. *Outcome-based education: Critical issues and answers*. Arlington, Va.: American Association of School Administrators.

Taba, H. 1966. Teaching strategies and cognitive functioning in elementary school children. Cooperative Research Project No. 2404. San Francisco State College.

Vygotsky, L. S. 1978. *Mind in society*. Cambridge, Mass.: Harvard University Press.

Walker, M., and Walker K. 1990. Instructional communication in the televised classroom: The effects of system design and teacher immediacy on student learning and satisfaction. *Communication Education* 39, 196–206.

Warschauer, M., and S. Lepeintre. 1997. Freire's dream or Foucault's nightmare: Teacher–student relations on an international computer network. In *Language learning through social computing*, edited by R. Debski, J. Gassin, and M. Smith, 67–89. Parkville, Australia: Applied Linguistics Association of Australia.

Wear, Bill. 2000. A handbook for mentors. At www.telementor.org/mise/info/mentoring_handbook.html (accessed March 2001).

Wenger, E. 1998. *Communities of practice: Learning, meaning, and identity*. Cambridge: Cambridge University Press.

———. 2000. Communities of practice: Stewarding knowledge. In *Knowledge horizons: The present and the promise of knowledge*, edited by C. Despres and D. Chauvel. Boston: Butterworth-Heinemann.

Wiggins, Grant P. 1998. *Educative assessment: Designing assessments to inform and improve student performance*. San Francisco: Jossey-Bass.

Wiggins, Grant P., and Jay McTighe. 1998. *Understanding by design*. Alexandria, Va.: Association for Supervision and Curriculum Development. At ubd.exchange.org.

Wiley, D. A. 2000. Connecting learning objects to instructional design theory: A definition, a metaphor, and a taxonomy. In *The instructional use of learning objects: Online version*, edited by D. A. Wiley. At reusability.org/read/chapters/wiley.doc (accessed October 2002).

Wilson, S. B. J. 1999. Teacher learning and the acquisition of professional knowledge: An examination of research on contemporary professional development. In *Review of Research in Education*, eds. A. Iran-Nejad and P. D. Pearson. Washington, D.C.: American Educational Research Association, 173–209.

Note: I am very grateful to all those who have contributed material and documents for this book from conversations and interviews with both faculty and students in the program to student evaluations, survey feedback, meeting notes, course assignments, and course and program Web sites. Material for portions of this book are drawn from the online courses I have taught entitled Introduction to Distributed Learning Environments; Learning and Technology; Curriculum and Technology; and Collaborative Action Research developed by M. Fisher, G. Stager, L. Polin, and T. Gray at Pepperdine University; and Survey of Technologies for Instruction; and Assessment and Information Management developed by M. Fisher, H. Shweizer, and J. Wipp at Marquette University, December 1997.

Index

About the Author

Mercedes Fisher, Ph.D., is co-director of the Online Master of Arts Program in Educational Technology at Pepperdine University in California and an Associate Professor in the Graduate School of Education and Psychology.

Dr. Fisher teaches both face-to-face and Web-based educational-technology courses. She has designed, developed, and delivered learning environments for several universities. Her expertise lies in educational technology, teaching, and training on the Web, designing collaborative learning models in Web-based environments, project-based learning, and knowledge management. She has published research articles in international journals and presented her research as an invited speaker at various international meetings and conferences. Dr. Fisher was named Fulbright Senior Specialist Scholar in 2002. Prior to joining Pepperdine, she was a three-time Distinguished Scholar at Marquette University. She takes pride in her teaching and brings her own special curiosity, genuine positive attitude, compassion, and successful experiences to the classroom. Recently, she has worked with grants from Microsoft Corporation, the U.S. Department of Education, Technology Literacy Challenge, and Wisconsin Department of Public Instruction. In 1997, she was selected as an International Group Study Exchange Team Member to study the development of online teaching and learning resources in Denmark and Germany. Prior to her experience at Marquette, she taught at the University of Southern Colorado and received both the

Outstanding Faculty Award and the Faculty Advisor of the Year for the 1995–96 school year. She also served as the Director of the Beck-Ortner Technology Center and conducted research emphasizing instructional design and technology applied to classroom learning.